tw-eat

a little book
with big feelings
and short recipes
for very busy lives

@professor_dave
David K. Smith

Copyright © 2020 David K. Smith

All rights reserved.

Cover design by David K. Smith

Book design by David K. Smith

No part of this book can be reproduced in any form or by written, electronic or mechanical, including photocopying, recording, or by any information retrieval system without written permission in writing by the author.

Published by David K. Smith

Printed by Amazon on Demand

Although every precaution has been taken in the preparation of this book, the publisher and author assume no responsibility for errors or omissions. Neither is any liability assumed for damages resulting from the use of information contained herein.

ISBN 979-8-570291-27-0

In memory of Sam

and for the future of the 7yo

CONTENTS

WHY TWITTER EATS? 4
SIMPLE SUPPERS – MEAT 7
SIMPLE SUPPERS – FISH 33
SIMPLE SUPPERS – VEG 46
A QUICK TEA 58
SATURDAY INDULGENCES 68
SUNDAY ROASTS... 79
CAKES and PUDDINGS 88
A LITTLE LONGER.. 104
AFTERS 113
INDEX 116

WHY TWITTER EATS?

My husband, Sam, loved good food and cooking. A famous family story told by his Mum, recalls the time that on a primary school trip to France, he was the only one of the kids who would try raw oysters – he ended up eating the lot. The last holiday we went on together was a night of luxury, and a fabulous meal, at Raymond Blanc's *Le Manoir aux Quat'Saisons* – visiting had been a life ambition of his. Even though he was almost too ill to walk from our room to the restaurant, when the beautiful plates of food arrived, his face lit up, and we talked animatedly into the small hours over many a glass of wine. Sam had cystic fibrosis, and when he eventually died aged 39, as a result of rejection of the lung transplant that had given him an extra 8 years of life, I was bereft. I was also a single dad to our then 6-year-old son.

Food had always been one of the threads that held us together as a family – we both loved to cook. From the time we first adopted our son, we had always shared family meals. Our food 'ground rules' were simple – we all tried new things together, only positive things would be said about food, and if something got left on the plate, so be it (there was always an extra slice of toast that could be found if someone needed to fill up later on). Our son turned into an enthusiastic and adventurous eater. After Sam's death, food has been a vital thread that has helped us both keep going.

As well as being a single dad – a full time job in itself – I also work. I therefore needed simple recipes to easily feed myself and a hungry growing boy. Indeed, after becoming a widower, cooking was a sort of therapy for me. In addition, my son is at his most settled and happy when he sees me busy in the kitchen, cooking something (hopefully) delicious to eat, with him joining in where possible.

I started tweeting what I was cooking. First and foremost, I did this for myself, as a way of recording the things I had cooked that I thought were good, so that I could make them again. Partly it was to show my friends and family that yes, we were surviving, and I was managing to put food on the table. And partly it was a way of sharing the recipes with my online friends. In order to tweet the recipes, I condensed them to 280 characters in such a way that someone with modest cooking skills should be able to reproduce them.

I really wanted to collect together some of my favourites twitter-eats (tw-eats) into a book for easy reference. The things I cook are mostly simple – I have a busy life. However, the now 7-year-old (7yo) and I have been through a lot – many of the recipes therefore deliver big in terms of comfort, and some are designed to look impressive for minimal effort. There are quick cooks and slow cooks in here, but in every case, they are briefly described in the form of a tweet. In some cases, I have broken a longer recipe down into 2 or 3 tweets, especially for the sections on Saturday indulgences, Sunday roasts, and some of the more special dishes towards the end of the book.

In general, unlike my original tweets, for the purposes of the book, I have given precise quantities – this may extend some recipes just a little beyond 280 characters – please forgive me. In places where you can use your judgement, or personal preference, I have left quantities vaguer. The quantities are for 2 adults (or 1 adult and a very hungry 7yo, with seconds). Cooking temperatures are all for a fan oven – if you don't have fan, or have gas, add 20°C and convert. The recipes are very short, so I have dispensed with ingredient lists and simply *italicised the ingredients* in the recipe itself – it should hopefully still be easy to make sure you have what you need.

I have occasionally added some extra words to clarify things for the less confident cook or suggest tweaks and modifications to the recipes. Most importantly, however, I use these extra words to tell you our story, and what the food means to us. As recipes worm their way into the life of a family, they take on emotional resonance far beyond the simple combination of ingredients on the plate. This is what I really want to capture in this book – little recipes but big feelings.

During the Coronavirus crisis, as restaurants and coffee shops closed, I found myself cooking even more from home, and wanting to cook some of the things we might have previously gone out to enjoy. I think we have all become more interested in home cooking, and food as therapy. At least I had a beautiful place to cook in. When Sam and I bought the house that was to be our forever home, the kitchen sold us on it – a large handsome room with a table at its heart. On becoming adoptive dads, and being joined by our special, caring, funny little boy, the kitchen became the focus of family life. All of us loved to spend time here – cooking drinking, talking, laughing. It is the room I live in. I wouldn't change it for the world.

In terms of work, I am a Professor of Chemistry. I manage a research team, teach students and am passionate about making science a more diverse & inclusive endeavour. I have always said that my alternative career would have been as a chef. I really admire *Michael O'Hare* from *The Man Behind the Curtain* – one of our favourite restaurants. Just like him, when I lead my team, I help innovate and design the experiments (creating recipes), check things are done properly (kitchen management) and help my team present their achievements to the world (final dishes going into the restaurant). Putting this book together has been a joy and allowed me to indulge in my fantasy job.

It is important to say I am just a cook, and this is just a collection. Many of the recipes were not designed by me – they are borrowed and adapted from the pages of my favourite cookbooks. I try to acknowledge these where relevant, but must highlight three of my muses: Nigel Slater, Nigella Lawson and Diana Henry. I admire the fact that none of them are 'chefs' – they are all, first and foremost, writers, who happen to love food and cooking. As writers, and unlike many chefs, they are not scared to cut a corner, or do something simple, if it tastes good. They inspire me with their words and have done more to teach my family how to love food than I can ever express. In some cases, my only contribution is to strip back the elegance of their words into the form of a bare-bones tweet, tell you why I love the food and explain what it means to me and my family.

I hope you enjoy the collection and the journey it takes you on. If not, at least I have created a family cookbook for me and the 7yo to use and treasure, that we can both dip into, to explore the memories and food inspiration it holds within.

David Smith

SIMPLE SUPPERS – MEAT

CHORIZO and CHICKPEA STEW

Fry 100g sliced *cured chorizo* in a dry pan until red oil runs out.

Add 2 sliced cloves *garlic*, chopped *onion*, fry.

Add 100ml *red wine*, reduce 50%.

Add can *chopped tomatoes*, *thyme*, simmer 20 min.

Add water if needed.

Add can drained *chickpeas*, simmer 10 min.

Serve with chopped *parsley*.

I first met Sam in 2006. Having known him for a little while (it's complicated don't ask!), I finally asked him to become my boyfriend in a Spanish restaurant in Leeds. This dish takes me straight back there. In the years that followed, Spain also became one of our favourite places to visit. This simple stew is just the kind of thing you might hope to get in any good Spanish tapas bar. Scaled up like this, and served with lots of crusty bread, it makes a simple, but delicious supper. It's equally good with butter beans or cannellini beans instead of the chickpeas.

PROFESSOR DAVE's STEAK FRITES

🐦 Season *steak*, rub with *olive oil*.

Cook on hot griddle to liking, turn 90° halfway through each side. Rest.

Fry *mushrooms* in butter, add generous *black pepper*, pinch *salt*, good shake *Worcester sauce*, 1tsp *Dijon mustard*, 50ml *single cream*, knob *butter* & juice from rested steak.

👤 When I first met Sam, I could basically cook, but I didn't love it. It was Sam who loved food and cooking and fired my passion for it – sharing food with him was just the most fun you could have. Back in those earliest days, the first time he came to my house, I really wanted to impress him, so this is what I cooked. The secrets are simple. Choose ribeye if you want soft, buttery luxury steak, rump if you want more texture. Both have the best flavour – far better than sirloin or fillet. Season the steak well with salt and pepper – use a fancy salt if you want. Then cook it exactly how the other person wants it – cooking steak is an act of love. Fries should be deep fried, crisp & golden. I just stick frozen French fries in the deep fat fryer – buy the ones with the least possible coating on, naked if possible. You then just need a really good sauce. Dinner in 10 minutes and Sam's heart won for ever.

SAFFRON & CHILLI GRILLED CHICKEN

🐦 Marinade 4 boneless *chicken thighs* in 4tbsp *olive oil*, juice of 1 *lemon*, 1 chopped *red chilli*, handful *mint*, 2 *garlic cloves* & large pinch *saffron*.

Cook on medium hot griddle, 8-10 min.

Serve with warm *couscous, preserved lemon, sultanas & parsley*.

Drizzle with *mint yoghurt, red chilli & mint*.

👤 The first holiday I ever went on with Sam was to Morocco. The smell, taste and look of this dish remind me of walking round the night-time food market in Marrakesh, the 'Jemaa el Fna', and just wanting to eat everything. It was exotic, it was exciting. This dish is not quite the 'real Morocco', but it evokes it, and is really enjoyed by the 7yo, as long as I hold back a bit on the chilli. Thinking back to that holiday, we hired a 'car' (a story in itself) and drove south over the Atlas Mountains until the road essentially ran out, continuing on camels deep into the Sahara Desert where we slept under starlight. It was probably insanely risky for someone like Sam, with cystic fibrosis, but it was completely unforgettable, and honestly, if you don't grab those moments in life, what are you doing?

PORK TONKATSU

🐦 Bash *pork steak*, dip in seasoned *flour*, then *egg*, then *panko breadcrumbs*.

Fry in 1cm *sunflower oil* until golden brown, 6-8 min.

Slice. Serve with boiled *rice* (optional: sprinkle *Shichimi Togarashi*), shredded *white cabbage* and *Bulldog Tonkatsu sauce*.

👤 I adore Japan, and so did Sam – it has a unique marriage of vibrant modern pop culture and historical elegance. My ultimate Japanese comfort food is Pork Tonkatsu. Like Japan itself, it's a perfect marriage between 'in-your-face' crowd-pleasing crispy fried pork with sweet sticky sauce, and the cleansing, understated elegance of simple plain rice and crisp cool cabbage. I like it so much, I've even learned how to make my own Tonkatsu sauce for those emergency moments when I can't find any 'Bulldog' sauce. (Homemade *Tonkatsu Sauce*: 2tbsp *tomato ketchup*, 2tbsp *Worcester sauce*, 1tsp *soy sauce*, ½tsp *sugar*). I use a meat thermometer so the pork is perfect – although you will know as soon as you slice it.

I actually proposed to Sam in the evocative old wooden ryokan in Hakone that you can see in the photograph. We had a beautiful, elegant kaiseki dinner served to us in our room. Afterwards, we were sat just there, overlooking a babbling river, and I got down on one knee – the perfect marriage indeed.

COFFEE-BRINED PORK CHOP

🐦 Make 500 ml *strong coffee*, add 15g *salt* & 3tbsp *dark sugar*.

Marinade 2 *pork chops* all day.

Dry.

Fry 8-10 minutes in *butter* & *oil*.

Serve with jacket *sweet potato* & sweetcorn. Chilli *butter* is good.

👤 This doesn't necessarily sound promising – I wasn't that convinced coffee had a place in savoury cooking when I read the original *Diana Henry* recipe. But it turns out this is a real cowboy-inspired classic – make a big pot of coffee in the morning, pour the leftovers over the meat while you are out rounding up cattle. With the all-American sides of sweet potato and corn it just works and puts a smile on your face.

The first holiday Sam and I had after his successful lung transplant in 2011 took us out to the Western USA – Las Vegas, Monument Valley, The Grand Canyon and Death Valley. We made a spectacular road trip, feeling the freedom of the wide-open spaces and exploring the incredible National Parks and reservations. This recipe takes me straight back to that 'Wild West' landscape, made all the sweeter by the fact that when I actually first had this dish, Sam cooked it for me.

PORK RAMEN

🐦 Heat 750ml *good stock*, sliced *ginger, spring onion, star anise*, 15 min.

Meanwhile, boil 2 *eggs* (8 min) & 'cook' *rice noodles*.

Strain stock, add 1tbsp *soy sauce*, 1tbsp *mirin*, 1tsp *sesame oil*, heat 5 min.

Add chopped *spring onion, spinach, sliced roast pork,* 1 min.

Add *cooked noodles*, top with halved *egg*.

👤 One of the 7yo's favourite meals – every time we are in London, he wants to visit a very cool place in Soho for Ramen. Sam would have heartily approved. However, it must be said this specific recipe is only a simple supper – making proper ramen is a true, and time-consuming, art form – this barely scratches the surface. Like ramen, however, this recipe is hugely versatile – change the vegetables (*chard* or *beansprouts* are good) or add *miso paste* to change the flavour profile.

One of my best memories from travelling in Japan with Sam was a day in Takayama when the rain was simply torrential. Having hiked round half the town and got thoroughly drenched, we found a tiny little place for ramen. Although the restaurant itself was humble, the steaming bowls of ramen were anything but – reviving and sustaining us in an almost magical way.

YOUTUBER's LAMB and MINT CURRY

Fry 1 *onion* in *sunflower oil* until brown, 15 min.

Add diced *lamb*, brown.

Chop & add 2 cloves *garlic*, 15g *ginger*, 1 *green chilli*.

Add 2tsp *coriander*, 1tsp *turmeric*, 1tsp *cumin*, 1tsp *yellow mustard seeds*, *black pepper*, *salt*, fry 2 min.

Add ½ can *chopped tomatoes*, 200ml water, simmer 1 h.

Add *peas*. Finish with *mint*.

I have a YouTube chemistry channel – *professordaveatyork*. A long time ago, I cooked a lamb curry on video to explain some of the science behind curry spices. Although the chemistry was fine, the curry, in all honesty, wasn't very good. In the following years, I worked on the recipe, with Sam as a willing 'taster', and this is now my optimised version of a lamb and mint curry – taking the classic English combination, and trying to make it work in a spiced setting. Leftover roast lamb is perfect for this if you have it, just add it later (after the spices) and drop the cooking time to 20-30 min.

ROAST CHICKEN and MAYO

🐦 Season *whole chicken* well with *salt, pepper* & *olive oil*.

Roast, Fan 180, 20 min per 500g + 20 min.

Serve with warm *crusty bread, salted butter, dressed green salad* (*olive oil:balsamic vinegar*, 2:1) and *mayonnaise*.

👤 Although it takes time to roast the chicken, the actual effort involved in making this is basically zero. It really is as simple as a ready meal. I know it sounds middle class and pompous, but buy the best chicken you can - you really can taste the difference if a chicken has had a happier and more active life. It changes the quality of the meat – the legs are bigger and juicier, while the breast is less 'fluffy' and doesn't dry out the same.

This was Sam's favourite simple supper. Indeed, warm chicken and cool mayonnaise is a beautiful thing. Sam and I would sit across the table, carving bits off the chicken, drinking ice cold white wine, buttering bread and talking, talking talking... Now I kind of do it with the 7yo. He mostly talks to *Alexa* – she can tell good jokes – it's not the same, but it helps us both through.

QUAIL EGG, BLACK PUDDING and BEETROOT SALAD

🐦 Boil 6 *quail eggs*, 2 min 20 sec, peel.

Fry chunks of *black pudding* in *oil*, 5 min.

Heat 25g *sugar*, 25ml *water*, *hazelnuts* until caramelised.

Cut *cooked beetroot* in wedges, add mixed leaves.

Dress: 2tbsp *olive oil*, 1tbsp *cider vinegar*, 1tbsp *honey*, 1tbsp *Dijon mustard*, *salt* & *pepper*.

👤 Who says salads should be light? The 7yo is not the biggest fan of salads, but this is the kind of salad he will happily demolish. To be fair, it has everything you could possibly want – crunchy, soft, sweet, sour, earthy, rich. Ideal served with a hunk of warm bread, thickly spread with butter, at the end of a very bad day. Just be warned, never was so much pain hidden away so easily in four little letters, 'peel' – but it's worth it for the end result.

PARTRIDGE with BLACKBERRIES and JUNIPER

🐦 Mix crushed *juniper berries*, *butter*, *salt* & *pepper*, rub *partridge*, wrap with *streaky bacon*.

Roast, Fan 180, 20 min, remove bacon into roasting tin, roast 5-10 min more.

Slice *parsnip*, fry in *oil*.

Mix steamed *cabbage* through *mash*.

Heat 50ml *port*, knob *butter*, handful *blackberries* & reduce.

👤 Our butcher has amazing game in season, and partridge at the very start of the season is my absolute favourite – sweet, juicy and delicious. Blackberries are also seasonal at the same time, so the marriage just seems perfect. This dish was always cooked at least once every Autumn when Sam was here – a seasonal ritual. Served with parsnip 'crisps' it becomes a special occasion quick meal (albeit unlike most recipes in the book, this is quite a hard-working 30 minutes).

I'm assuming for the recipe you know how to make mash. The secrets are drying the potatoes in a hot pan after they've boiled to softness, putting them through a ricer for extra smoothness, and then being generous with butter, milk, salt & pepper.

GRILLED SUMAC LAMB and PITTA CHIPS

🐦 Marinate *lamb chops* in *garlic, olive oil, lemon juice, thyme.*

Soak thin-sliced *cucumber* in 25ml water, 25ml *white wine vinegar,* 1tbsp *caster sugar.*

Mix *yoghurt* & *mint.*

Put 7yo old to bed, 30 min.

Sprinkle chops with *sumac.* Griddle 3-4 min a side.

Slice *pitta bread*, deep fry 1 min, season.

Serve with *sumac.*

👤 This is the kind of supper I make for myself when it's been a horrendous day, and I just want to get the 7yo into bed, relax with a glass of wine and escape into my Kindle (one of my most precious possessions). Lamb chops are perfect for this kind of cooking – they take no time to cook, but always manage to feel like an indulgent treat. It's also easy to get flavour into them very quickly. This recipe is simple, and the 'pitta chips' are a total revelation – maybe it's just the truth that you can deep fry anything and make it taste delicious!

CHICKEN and CAULIFLOWER CHEESE

🐦 In roasting dish: *chicken thighs* (skin-on, bone-in), *cauliflower florets*, quartered *new potatoes*, halved *banana shallots*, sprigs of *thyme*, *olive oil*, *salt & pepper*.

Roast, Fan 180, 35 min.

Grate *parmesan* all over.

Roast for final 10 min.

👤 Traybakes are my favourite kind of cooking – just so easy. I mean honestly, why would you bother with shop-bought ready meals? This is not the most colourful dish, but for comforting flavours on a winter's evening, it's hard to beat. This is the ideal kind of thing to cook on a school night and means I can help the 7yo do some reading or play a game while he waits. Alternatively, it just gives me a bit more time to clear up the trail of destruction he creates every time he gets home.

DUCK & APRICOT WRAPS

🐦 Season and prick 2 *duck legs*. Slow roast, Fan 150, 90 min.

Shred *duck legs*. Add to segments of ripe *apricots*.

Dress: 2 tbsp *olive oil*, 1 tbsp *lime juice*.

Finish with *coriander* & *red chilli* and serve on warm *tortillas*.

👤 Ignore the oven for 90 minutes and then assemble something that is both beautiful and delicious – it's actually easier than one of those well-known branded tortilla kits. This recipe is totally compatible with being a single parent yet will make you feel like you're a million dollars. And what kids don't enjoy wraps? The apricots must be perfectly ripe, soft and fragrant, because they aren't getting any cooking. That makes this a delicious summer dish – as soon as you find perfect apricots, then go for it, you won't regret it!

PIGEON, BEETROOT and HAZELNUT SALAD

Prepare salad with blanched *mange tout*, chopped *cooked beetroot*, *cucumber*, *hazelnuts* and *crisp leaves*.

Dress: 2tbsp *olive oil*, 1tbsp *cider vinegar*, 1tbsp *honey*, 1tbsp *grain mustard*, *salt* & *pepper*

Season *pigeon breast*, fry in oil & butter, 2 min each side.

Slice & serve on dressed salad.

Probably the most commonly asked question on Twitter is 'How on earth do you get the 7yo to eat that?' Firstly, I'm lucky! He does genuinely love food. But secondly, we have always pushed his palate, while never making a fuss about food. Food has always been a big topic of conversation, and only ever talked about it in positive terms – what we like, how it tastes etc. I also carefully and strategically choose ingredients. In this case beetroot is one of his top favourites (I actively seek out beetroot recipes), mange tout and cucumber are also favourites of his, pigeon was new and he loved it, while the leaves and hazelnuts he didn't like and largely left (no fuss – we just try it together and talk about what it tastes like). Of course, a honey mustard dressing helps! There is then always some sort of fallback that he can fill up with – in this case lots of crusty bread.

BBQ CHIP-CHOS 1331

Chop & try 4 *spring onions*, 1 *red chilli*, left-over *roast chicken*.

Stir through 1tbsp *BBQ sauce* & 50g grated *cheese* until melted.

Serve over *french fries*.

Add *sour cream*, *red chillies*, grated *cheese* & *BBQ sauce* to taste.

From a light, healthy pigeon salad, to sheer, filthy indulgence! There's a bar in York – 1331 – that invented 'chip-chos'. Essentially, they are Nachos, but with the tortilla chips replaced by french fries. In 1331, they come with all the traditional Mexican toppings – beef chilli, guacamole, salsa, sour cream, cheese (do try it, it's great). I decided to take the idea in a spicy barbecue direction as a way of using up some leftover roast chicken. It's phenomenal!

1331 is a special place for us as a family. You can hire the upstairs rooms, and it has marked some of the key points in our lives. When we formally adopted the 7yo, we had the celebration party there. When we scattered some of Sam's ashes at his memorial bench in Museum Gardens, it's where friends and family went afterwards for a drink and a chat. Irrespective of the occasion, we always make sure there's a big pile of chip-chos!

ICELANDIC LAMB CHOPS

🐦 Cube *potatoes, season*, toss in *olive oil*. Roast, Fan 180, 30-40 min.

Roast *red pepper* in olive oil. Fan 180, 20-30 min. Remove skin, mash with *feta*, a trickle of olive oil & a squeeze *lemon* juice.

Season *lamb chops* with *Icelandic lava salt & pepper*. Griddle, 3-4 min a side.

👤 We had a wonderful family holiday in Iceland. One meal really sticks in the memory. After a long day exploring the magical glaciers & ice fields of Eastern Iceland, we returned to the farmstead where we were staying, and they served us their own lamb. It was simply done, but absolutely delicious. Here, I seasoned the lamb with Icelandic 'lava salt' to help evoke the memory, but any good salt will do. Vegetables  are often imported in Iceland, so I don't feel guilty about serving the lamb up with Greek-style roasted red peppers. The 'parmentier potatoes' are a mainstay in our house. They are a super-easy side dish with minimal effort, delivering crunchy, crispy, roasty, toasty edges and soft insides. They can be further improved by adding rosemary or a clove of garlic.

'JERUSALEM' CHICKEN

Peel & quarter *Jerusalem artichokes*. Boil in water with a squeeze *lemon juice*, 10 min. Drain.

Add to 4 *chicken thighs*, 6 halved *shallots*, 3 cloves sliced *garlic*, 1 sliced *lemon*, 2tsp *crushed pink peppercorns*, big pinch *saffron*, *thyme*, *tarragon*, *salt*, 3tbsp *olive oil*, 2tbsp *water*.

Marinade as long as you can.

Roast, Fan 180, 45 min.

I adore this dish and the 7yo just about tolerates it – in honesty, Jerusalem artichokes are at the very limit of what I can serve him, although he is always more tempted to try them when I tell him they make you fart. It's a very easy traybake, prepared with minimum effort and tastes amazing. The recipe is adapted from *Yotam Ottolenghi's* Jerusalem cookbook. Every February, when Jerusalem artichokes come into season, and there is so little other good local seasonal produce, I just have to cook it. I serve this dish with a good sourdough bread, so the 7yo has plenty to fill up with.

DUCK and CANNELINI BEANS

🐦 Season & slash *duck breast*.

Fry in dry pan, medium heat skin side down, 5 min. Flip, 1 min.

Drain can *cannellini beans*, place in small roasting dish with *rosemary* & glug of *dry marsala wine*.

Put duck on top, breast side up. Roast, Fan 180, 15 min.

Partly mash the *cannellini beans* & serve.

👤 Duck breast makes a very fast supper and is one of my go-to meals after a hard day, when I decide I want to eat on my own, with the 7yo tucked up in bed, just to de-stress. This way of cooking duck breast (5 min in pan, 15 min in oven) is a bomb-proof way of getting pink juicy delicious meat and perfect crisp skin, turning it into a real hero ingredient. I also like to serve duck breast on lentils (whisper it quietly – I quite like microwaveable packets of ready-prepared lentils as a simple base for a duck breast). A glass of Pinot Noir is an essential accompaniment – just make sure you haven't already drunk too much of the bottle beforehand while de-stressing.

STU's HEALING ITALIAN CHICKEN MEATBALL PASTA

Take *Italian chicken sausages* ('Chicken Italia', *Heck*) out of skins.

Form small meatballs, fry till brown, remove.

Gently fry fine-diced *onion/carrot/celery* till soft. Add chopped *garlic*.

Add *can tomatoes, Italian herbs*, chicken meatballs, *black olives*.

Heat, season, add to *pasta*.

In Sam's final days, when his transplanted lungs were rejecting, after the 8 fantastic years of extra life they had given him, he was hospitalised on the cystic fibrosis ward in Leeds. The ward is amazing, with caring and dedicated staff who really understand CF patients and their families. They essentially let me live on a sofa bed in his hospital room. Probably the best thing I ate in the month I spent there was brought in by Sam's brother, Stuart. It was a simple pasta dish in a Tupperware container that I could microwave up in the ward kitchen. After endless days of ready meals and Costa sandwiches it just tasted great – proper soul food. I have cooked it often since and thought of the comfort it brought me in such a difficult time.

CHICKEN and MUSHROOM PIE

🐦 Fry sliced *mushrooms* until reduced.

Chop *leftover roast chicken*.

Melt 25g *butter*, add 25g *flour*, 250ml *chicken stock*, 50ml *milk*, salt & *pepper*.

Place ingredients in 20cm pie tin, pour white sauce over.

Top with *puff pastry*, trim, decorate. Brush with beaten *egg*.

Bake, Fan 180, 30 min.

👤 After a roast chicken (pages 15 & 85), I often make a chicken pie to use up the leftovers (with *chicken stock* made from the carcass – let it simmer for an evening with *bay leaf, parsley stalks*, 2 *peppercorns*, ½ *onion* and *carrot*). I prefer the pie with mushrooms, but *sweetcorn* is also good (just open a can, drain and tip it in). If you are feeling more ambitious, make your own *shortcrust pastry* (rub 110g flour, 25g lard, 25g butter, & salt; add 1-2 tbsp water; leave 30 min in fridge, roll).

I always used to decorate the top of the pie with a message, but for some reason stopped, and forgot all about it. Then one day, the 7yo said 'You never put messages on your pies anymore – is it because Pop died?'. So, I made him this pie specially. Pies are always made with love, but I think they taste even better when they say it on the top!

CHICKEN and CHICKPEA MADRAS PIE

Chop 1 *onion*, 1 clove *garlic*, 15g *ginger*.

Gently fry *onion* until soft, then add *garlic*, *ginger* and 1 tbsp *Madras curry powder* and fry 2 min more.

Add chopped *roast chicken*, drained can *chickpeas*, place in pie tin.

Make *white sauce* and pour over as on previous page.

Finish pie as before.

A simple, tasty, slightly crazy, very basic 'East meets West' adaptation of the standard pie recipe on the previous page and a gateway dish designed to get the 7yo interested in eating Indian food. I grew up as a huge fan of Stockport County, going to Friday night matches with my dad. Nowadays, the Balti Pie is a staple at football grounds across the North West – consider this a home-made homage to the mighty 'boys in blue' (sadly now somewhere close to the bottom of the football pyramid). Serve with buttered steamed cabbage with caraway seeds stirred through at the end and maybe some naan bread to mop up the Madras-spiced sauce.

DUCK LEG with SWEET & SOUR CRANBERRIES

Season and prick *duck leg*. Roast, Fan 150, 90 min.

Cube *potatoes*, season, toss in *sunflower oil*. Roast, Fan 150, 60 min.

Take 25g dried *cranberries*, 100ml *red wine*, 1 tbsp *red wine vinegar*, 2tsp *sugar*. Simmer & reduce to a sticky sauce.

Use good *salad dressing* (I buy Mary Berry's 'Classic') on *leaves*.

An easy luxurious supper that I sometimes have if the 7yo is away at his grandparents and have some time to myself. I will be catching up on my favourite podcasts (my kitchen is strictly a TV-free zone), and relaxing. Other than opening and closing an oven door, mixing a few things in a pan and leaving to simmer, there really is nothing to it. In this case, because the 'parmentier potatoes' are cooked alongside the duck they are at a lower temperature than those on page 23, so they get longer in the oven. The dressed leaves here were lamb's lettuce – I love their mild softness. If you wanted something with more character, then watercress dressed in olive oil and balsamic vinegar would be fantastic and add a touch of bitterness to counteract the sweet & sour sauce.

ITALIAN MEATBALL & FENNEL SPAGHETTI

🐦 Take *Italian fennel sausage* out of casings, make into meatballs, fry till brown.

Fine dice *fennel* & *onion*, fry till soft. Add *garlic*.

Add ½ can *chopped tomatoes*, meatballs & splash *red wine*.

Cook 15 min.

Serve through cooked *spaghetti* with *parmesan*.

👤 We are lucky that on our local high street, the award-winning 'Bishy Road' there's an amazing Sicilian café, and even luckier that the owner Beppe, sells sausages made to his mother's recipe. Beppe has always been a good friend to Sam, me and the 7yo – he currently chairs the Bishy Road Traders' Association and embodies the true meaning of local community. His sausages are a 'hero ingredient' and can elevate any dish to the next level. Buy some of his amazing ice cream while you are there, and you can do the same to pudding (see page 96). You are then ideally placed to create one of the simplest, but tastiest two-course meals you will ever cook.

GNOCCHI with STEAK and ASPARAGUS

Boil ready-made *gnocchi*, 1-2 min.

Boil/steam *asparagus*, 2-3 min

Fry *steak* rare. Rest.

Add gnocchi & a knob of *butter* to steak juices in pan, fry 3 min.

Make dressing: 3tbsp *olive oil*, 1½ tbsp *lemon juice, basil, parmesan, garlic.*

Plate gnocchi. Add sliced steak & asparagus. Dress.

There are days when you just want a taste of luxury but don't want to make any effort. This takes 10 minutes from start to finish and with two luxury ingredients on the one plate feels like a real treat (you can make one good-sized steak stretch between two people). I had a version of this on the day they announced that the first Coronavirus vaccine looked like it worked! Frying the gnocchi in the juices in the steak pan is not essential, but it really takes the dish to the next level as they soak up all that flavour and get a toasty, crisp golden exterior.

BARBECUED HOT DOGS

🐦 Slice 1 *onion*, gently fry in *sunflower oil* until golden brown.

Barbecue *good sausages* until cooked through & slightly charred.

Serve in the best roll you can – ideally a *brioche hot dog roll*.

Add *French's yellow mustard* & *Heinz tomato ketchup*.

👤 This really doesn't need a recipe, but it's what I want on a lazy hot summer day, and it captures something essential about our family eating. The true masters of the barbecue are Ann & Ian, Sam's parents, who regularly host incredible barbecues in their back garden, very much-loved by the 7yo and his cousins. They spend all day producing an amazing array of tasty dishes. I can't compete!

More importantly, however, hot dogs take me right back to one of my happiest afternoons – sitting with Sam watching baseball at the San Francisco Giants in the blazing afternoon sunshine, with a fabulous view out over the bay. We gorged on junk food – nachos, hot dogs, the works – and enjoyed a game in which the Giants had a great come-from-behind victory against the Philadelphia Phillies. This was the season that the Giants went on a month or so later to win the World Series. Sam wasn't really a fan of sport at all, but he loved baseball – sitting in a bar with great food, plenty of beer and a ball game on was one of our favourite ways to spend an evening in America. That afternoon sits in my memory like a blazing star – every time I taste a hot dog done perfectly, with care and love, I'm there.

SIMPLE SUPPERS – FISH

MOULES MARINIERE

🐦 Clean *fresh mussels*, discard broken ones or ones that stay open if tapped.

Chop 2 *shallots* & 1 clove *garlic*, gently fry in *butter* in large pan.

Add mussels, 100ml *white wine*, put lid on.

Cook 4-5 min until mussels open.

Add 100ml *double cream*.

Finish with chopped *parsley*.

👤 Like father like son – my boys absolutely love(d) mussels. Hands-on, fingers-messy eating, it's surprisingly perfect for kids and a good way for encouraging children to become more adventurous eaters. If they don't like the mussels, they just fill up on bread and butter, dipping it in the creamy 'soup'! I love these two photos of Sam and the 7yo, taken almost 30 years apart. When I'm particularly exhausted at the end of a long day, I have been known to do 'Boil in the Bag' Moules Mariniere from a well-known supermarket. They are not quite as good as the real thing, but they still hit the spot for the 7yo.

COD TRICOLORE

🐦 Place 2 *cod fillets* in roasting tray with halved *cherry tomatoes*, *basil* leaves, torn *mozzarella*.

Season, grate *parmesan* over, drizzle with *olive oil*.

Bake, Fan 180, 15 min.

Serve with cubed *rosemary roast potatoes* (see page 23).

👤 Traybakes are a fantastic way to introduce kids to cooking. Why are we Brits so obsessed with teaching kids to bake cakes? They are not very healthy and it's not the best cooking life skill (unless you want to win the Bake Off). There is just as much pride (if not more) to be gained by children in cooking the dinner you are going to sit down and eat together. This is so quick and simple, looks beautiful, and the 7yo loves to steal some of the uncooked mozzarella and cherry tomatoes as he prepares it. The recipe is adapted from *Jamie Oliver* - I admire the way he's done so much to revolutionise British food culture.

MACKEREL, RHUBARB and CUCUMBER

Mix 2 sliced *shallots*, 1 tbsp *white wine vinegar*, 1 tbsp *olive oil*, 2 tsp *sugar*, *rhubarb* cut to 5 cm.

Roast, Fan 180, 10 min.

Lay *mackerel fillets* on top, roast 7 min.

Scatter *hazelnuts*, roast 5 min.

Serve with *crème fraiche*, sliced *cucumber* & *dill*, lots of *crusty bread*.

On holiday in Padstow down in Cornwall, Sam loved to go out on the early morning mackerel boats and catch some fish for lunch. Me, not so much – sea-sicknesses tended to keep me shoreside! Once, when we were there as a family, I got an urgent phone call from the boat as he headed off down the estuary to tell me he'd 'accidentally' got on the wrong boat, and he wasn't just going to be gone for 2 hours but would actually be out for most of the day. I'm sure I detected glee in his voice at the thought of a relaxing child-free day doing one of the things he liked best. At least he brought back plenty of fish for tea!

This Scandinavian-inspired dish is light and refreshing – perfect for summer. If your rhubarb is tough, it may need to cook a bit longer.

SOLE MEUNIERE with FRIES

Coat *sole fillets* in *seasoned flour*.

Fry in *butter & sunflower oil*, 2 min skin down, 1-2 min skin up. Rest.

Add 40g *butter* to pan, heat till brown & foaming.

Add *capers*, *chopped parsley* & a good squeeze of *lemon juice*.

Pour butter sauce over fish.

The 7yo loves fish and it is one of the simplest, fastest things you can cook. My fries have to be cooked in a proper deep fat fryer (see page 9) - I know it's probably not that healthy, but they just taste so much better than miserable oven chips. I remember in the early days of our relationship, one of the first things I bought for Sam when he moved into a new flat was a deep fat fryer. He thought I was mad – maybe I am – but a crisp bowl of salted rustling fries is total comfort food territory for me. Butter sauce and proper fries mean this dish isn't really in health food territory, but it's still lower in calories than a trip to the local chippy, and it tastes fab.

SALMON, FENNEL and DILL 'EN PAPILLOTE'

Par-boil *waxy potatoes*, 10 min. Cut in thick slices.

Melt 20g *butter*.

Place 1 portion sliced *potatoes*, sliced *fennel*, chopped *dill*, 10g melted *butter*, good squeeze *lemon* and 1tbsp *dry vermouth*, on greaseproof paper. Top with 1 thick *salmon* fillet. Wrap. Repeat for portion 2.

Bake, Fan 180, 25 min.

The best salmon I ever ate was sitting at a restaurant on the dock in Seattle, watching the boats come and go across the Puget Sound. It was the last holiday Sam and I took together before we adopted our son, and we squeezed out every last moment of grown-up indulgence. We loved the Pacific Northwest – the amazing food & drink culture, the beautiful wild landscapes, and the laid-back liberal people. It's a stunning and welcoming part of the USA where we just felt instantly at home. This recipe is a *Diana Henry* invention from her fabulous cookbook *Simple*.

SEA BASS TRAYBAKE

🐦 Slice *potatoes*, add *olive oil*, season. Roast, Fan 180, 25 min.

Fry *mushrooms, garlic, thyme*. Add squeeze *lemon*.

Slash *sea bass* skin, stuff with *basil, parsley, thyme*.

Mix mushrooms with potatoes. Lay fish on.

Roast, Fan 180, 10 min.

Serve with 2 tbsp *olive oil*, 1 tbsp *lemon, capers, parsley basil*.

👤 The 7yo and I got a rescue cat, Mittens (Mitts) – he is a massive fan of the days I cook fish. Sea bass is easy to cook and marries well with different flavours. This traybake, adapted from *Jamie Oliver*, served with 'Sauce Vierge', builds the dish on top of part-roasted sliced potatoes – if you want to make it fancier, use wild mushrooms.

This recipe is hugely adaptable – for example, change the mushroom mix for *red peppers, black olives & sliced lemon* to make the dish brighter and more spring/summer-like. Another good variation is *roast artichokes* from a jar & *herby/lemony marinated green olives*. The secret is to place the other ingredients into the roasting tray at the right time so that they will be cooked to your liking. As long as the fish gets 10 min on top at the end, and the potatoes have 30-40 min overall, you're winning. Essentially, it's a build it yourself ready meal.

SEARED TUNA 'NICOISE'

Plate warm boiled *green beans*, chopped *tomatoes* & *cucumber*.

Dress: 2tbsp *olive oil*, 1tbsp *lemon juice*, chopped *basil*, 1tbsp *grain mustard*.

On very hot griddle, sear oiled *tuna steak* 1 min each side, turning through 90° after 30 s.

Dress.

Serve with *fries* (unhealthy) or *crusty bread* (virtuous).

Sam loved tuna – ideally raw. This dish became a bit of a standard in our house, especially when we could sit out in the late afternoon sunshine in our little back yard. However, I would often annoy him by overcooking the tuna – so *really* don't hang about once it's in the pan. For the record, I know it's not really a niçoise – where are the *eggs*, *black olives* and *red onions*, what is the mustard doing, and why is there cucumber in there? (Answer: the 7yo loves cucumber). Feel free to tweak the recipe to get it just how you want it, but the version here is how we like it!

HERB-ROLLED SALMON

Cut *salmon* and roll in soft herbs (e.g. *dill, tarragon, parsley*).

Cut *courgette* into half-moons.

Cook *salmon* & *courgette* in pan with *butter* & a *little oil*, 5 min.

Add 2tbsp *creme fraiche* & *squeeze of lemon*.

Serve with fluffy, buttery *mashed potatoes*.

There's a time of year when we have a non-stop supply of courgettes coming from the allotment. This is probably my favourite way of using them up. The 7yo absolutely adores fish and mashed potato, so this ranks up there as one of his favourite dinners. Normally, I can't honestly be bothered making mash, but here, the fish is so simple that it's easy enough to get a good mash made on the side – as explained on page 17, I always use a potato ricer on boiled & dried potatoes for the smoothest mash possible, then add a generous amount of butter, milk, salt and pepper.

SAM's MEXICAN FISH STEW

Sea bass, clams, prawns, tomato, onion, jersey royals, radish, sweetcorn, ancho chillies, deep-fried *tortilla, coriander*.

Sam was a brilliant cook – the photograph shows him as a teenager cooking for his family, something he always loved to do. This Mexican Fish Stew is something he made in 2018, the year before he died. It was both beautiful and delicious. I don't exactly know how he made it, and I can't find the recipe, so I have merely listed the ingredients – that was all I have on my original tweet. I can, of course, reconstruct a vague idea of how he did it. Shellfish cooked in a tomato-stew base, warmed with ancho chillies, the fresh vegetables dropped in late-on to keep some crunch. The deep-fried tortillas, a pan-fried fillet of sea bass and a scattering of coriander being added at the very end. I'm sure I could recreate something quite like it – but it wouldn't be exactly the same. It's worth sharing that this is actually the perfect analogy of how it feels when you are bereaved – a series of individual flavours of memories float around in your head, but you aren't always quite sure how to connect them into a coherent whole.

WHITBY CRAB CAKES (and SWEETCORN RELISH)

For 6 small crab cakes.

Take 1 *dressed crab*, gently mix with big handful *panko breadcrumbs*, ½ *beaten egg*, squeeze of *mayo*, squeeze of *lemon juice*, chopped *parsley*, *salt* & *pepper*.

Put in fridge to firm up a little. Shape into small patties.

Fry gently in *sunflower oil* and *butter*.

The 7yo adores the seaside, and out on the East Coast of Yorkshire are some great places that we both love – Scarborough, Filey, Robin Hood's Bay. It's also the home of Whitby and its famous crab, some of the best in the UK. Sam adored crab and would always bring home a dressed crab whenever we went to the coast. It's a tradition I've continued, and crab cakes are something the 7yo and me both love to eat. Probably worth pointing out – that crab the 7yo caught is *not* a Whitby crab, it's just a little mud crab!

If you're interested, the sweetcorn relish in the photo is also cracking. (Sweetcorn Relish: fry 1 *shallot* till soft, add 2 cobs *fresh sweetcorn* kernels, chopped *red chilli*, 60ml *cider vinegar*, 25g *caster sugar* ½ tsp *mustard powder*, boil 10 min).

ITALIAN SEA BREAM

🐦 Fry sliced *spring onions*, *fennel*, *carrots* in *olive oil*, 4 min.

Add halved *cherry tomatoes*, 10 stoned *olives*, 2 cloves *garlic*, ½ *red chilli*, 2 min.

Score *sea bream*, stuff with *parsley* & *dill*, lay on top.

Add 150ml *white wine*, reduce by ½.

Add 300ml *water*, lid on, boil hard, 8min.

Serve with *lemon zest* & *herbs*.

👤 A good recipe for whole fish is always useful. Sea bream cooked on the bone is, in my opinion, one of the most flavourful white fish you can eat, and this *Jamie Oliver* recipe is a cracker. Just serve it with good crusty bread.

I wasn't sure about feeding it to the 7yo, and carefully took his fish off the bone, leaving the head and skeleton on the side. Needless to say, that was *all* he wanted to look at - he was fascinated with the bones, the brain, and wanted to eat the eyes. Next time he'll just get the whole thing on the plate and can do his own fish surgery.

SEA BASS, OLIVES and FENNEL

🐦 Fry 1 sliced *red onion*, 1 clove *garlic*, *rosemary leaves*, pinch *dried red chilli*.

Add 120ml *white wine*, reduce.

Add chopped *fresh tomatoes*, *kalamata olives*, *capers*.

Separately fry sliced *fennel* till coloured.

Combine, roast, Fan 150, 30 min.

Fry *sea bass*, 4 min skin down, 1 min skin up, serve on veg.

👤 I've never been to the Greek islands, but this is how I imagine they taste. It is a part of the world I definitely want to discover with the 7yo. Travel is a massive part of my life – I love adventure, culture and new experiences. Sharing them with someone is really special. Planning new places to go is one of the things that helps keep me going through bereavement and single parenthood. I think the combination of Ancient Greek culture, sun-kissed beaches and fabulous food will make for two very happy travellers in the years to come.

SIMPLE SUPPERS – VEG

'SMOKY' AUTUMN PASTA

🐦 Crush 1 clove *garlic* and fry in generous *butter*.

Add 200g dry *pasta*, 500ml *veg stock*, 200ml *milk* and *thyme*.

Bring to boil, simmer 15 min until 'saucy', with pasta al dente.

Add 60g soft/melty *smoked cheese* and *black pepper*.

Heat through, serve with more *black pepper*.

👤 This recipe is adapted from *Nigel Slater* and is the craziest way you will ever cook pasta! The pasta is cooked *in* the sauce, releasing its starch into what you eat – but it seriously works. I pair it with a crunchy pepper & cucumber salad with a sharp lemony salad dressing on the side for contrast. The flavour this delivers amazed me when I first cooked it. I was feeling really low at the time, missing adult dinnertime conversation and Sam's smiling face across the table. This dish was so comforting and warming, it was just like getting the big hug I was longing for and couldn't have.

SUMMER GNOCCHI SALAD

Boil *gnocchi*, 1-2 min.

Fry *gnocchi* in olive oil & butter until golden, then add chopped *garlic*.

Chop, slice and mix fridge-cold *heritage tomatoes*, *radishes*, *spring onions* & *parsley*.

Mix and serve.

The greengrocer on the local high street has the most amazing seasonal produce – they did me proud with the beautiful heritage tomatoes that are the making of this visually stunning *Nigel Slater* dish. This is a taste of summer on a plate, perfect for eating in the garden under the hot summer sun. It's a really interesting and unique way of presenting what is, essentially, a salad. I have to be honest; this dish was not the 7yo's favourite – he loves gnocchi, and they got demolished, but tomatoes and radishes are both towards the bottom of his list. Still, he was full, and I was happy.

HALLOUMI ROAST VEGETABLES

🐦 Roast mid-sized cubed *potato*, slightly larger cubed *sweet potato*, 2 bashed *garlic* cloves & *thyme* with *olive oil, salt & pepper*, Fan 180, 15 min.

Add *red onion* wedges, 15 min.

Add sliced *red & yellow peppers*, 15 min.

Add sliced *halloumi*, 10 min.

Serve

👤 As ever in a traybake, the secret is making sure everything has just the right amount of time in the oven. It takes an hour all in, but it's hardly high-intensity cooking – you can easily get on with other jobs while it does its thing. This is a really tasty dish – when I have shared it on Twitter it is clear that many people already have their own variants of this excellent recipe. My original inspiration for this particular combination was *Nigella Lawson*, but all kinds of other veg roasted, and topped with halloumi would taste great.

CHEESE & ONION TART

🐦 Gently fry 3-6 sliced *onions, thyme, salt, pepper* in 50g *butter* until soft.

Place *puff pastry* sheet on baking tray, add *onions* leaving 2cm border. Brush border with onion butter.

Add 100g *gruyere*. Sprinkle 25g parmesan on top.

Bake, Fan 200, 20 min.

Serve with *salad*.

👤 Shamelessly adapted from my hero *Nigel Slater*, even down to the fact that because it's photographed with beer in his cookbook, it always makes me crave a glass (as you can see). The tart is quite rich, so make sure you dress the salad with a sharp acidic dressing – I use an *olive oil* and *balsamic vinegar* mix, with plenty of *black pepper*. The basic concept of an open tart on shop-bought puff pastry is super-versatile. Put whatever you want on top, and as long as it bakes nicely in 20 minutes, that's dinner sorted. You can do a nice light version with *tomatoes, mozzarella* and *basil* that sends the whole thing in a pizza-tart direction.

KALE & CANNELLINI BEAN PASTA STEW

🐦 Fry chopped *bacon* (optional), then 1 chopped *onion* & *carrot*.

Add chopped *garlic* clove, 2tsp *tomato puree*, *thyme*.

Add *chicken stock* & *water* (750ml total). Boil.

Add can *cannellini beans* & 100g *pasta*, boil 5 min.

Add *kale*, simmer 7 min.

Season, stir in handful *parmesan*. Serve with *parmesan*.

👤 A great one pot pasta soup/stew recipe that is both filling and satisfying, this was a massive hit with the 7yo. The broth is seasoned by the parmesan – if you want to give it even more savour, drop a parmesan rind in with the pasta and lift it out at the end. You can probably get away without crusty bread, as this is a very hearty soup, but you might want some to help mop up the juices.

CAULIFLOWER CHEESE PASTA

Fry florets from 1 small *cauliflower* in 25g *butter* & 1tbsp *oil* till lightly golden.

Cook 200g *pasta*,

Add 150ml *double cream*, 100g *cheddar*, 50g *parmesan*, *black pepper*, heat.

Add pasta, top with *dill*, serve.

Kids always love pasta, and the 7yo is no exception. This dish is a mash-up of cauliflower cheese and macaroni cheese and is a nice way of getting vegetables enthusiastically eaten. An alternative approach is just to mix leftover cauliflower cheese with pasta, but in this recipe, I think the crisp fried cauliflower against the soft pasta and creamy cheese sauce is just fab. You may wonder why the cauliflower is fried in both butter and oil – in fact this is something I do a lot through the book. The butter is for flavour and browning, the oil is there to stop the butter burning. This recipe is adapted from *Nigel Slater* and exemplifies everything that is good about his simple, yet clever, flavour-filled cooking style.

HALLOUMI FINGERS and AUBERGINE MASH

🐦 Roast halved *aubergine* & 2 whole *garlic* cloves in *olive oil*, Fan 180, 45 min.

Scoop *aubergine* flesh, mash with soft *garlic* innards, add 1 tbsp *olive oil* & squeeze of *lemon*.

Cut *halloumi* fingers. Coat: *seasoned flour*, *egg*, *panko*. Fry till golden.

Scatter *pomegranate* seeds & *mint* leaves.

👤 Sam hated aubergines with a passion – he just wouldn't let me cook them, even though obviously, he never said this in front of the 7yo as it would have broken our 'family food rules'. Funnily enough, the 7yo also won't eat them. I hoped this *Nigel Slater* dish would convert him – it didn't, but I think it's absolutely delicious. Next time, I will keep the halloumi fingers but combine them with some mashed *beetroot* (roast *beetroot* in oil, then puree with a little *butter* and *crème fraiche*). On colour grounds I'd then have to drop the pomegranate – maybe throw in some toasted hazelnuts instead. Alternatively, I'll just serve the halloumi fingers with chips and beans.

MUSHROOM & SAGE GNOCCHI

Fry 2 chopped *shallots* in *butter*.

Add 200g *mixed mushrooms*, fry, season, add 50ml *white wine* & a few chopped *sage* leaves.

Fry *gnocchi* in *butter* till golden (no need to boil them).

Add *mushrooms* to *gnocchi*. Top with crispy fried *sage*.

There's nothing hugely innovative about this classic combination of flavours, which is pure comfort food for a damp foggy evening. But frying the gnocchi just elevates them to pure indulgence – the crisp golden exterior giving way to the soft, doughy, pillowy interior is perfection. Crispy sage leaves on the top finish it perfectly. This is the kind of supper the 7yo loves, and if he's been good, it's the kind of thing he gets to eat in front of his favourite Netflix cartoon.

BAKED CAMEMBERT and CRANBERRY

🐦 Take a *puff pastry* sheet on a baking sheet.

Spread a circle with *cranberry sauce*.

Place a '*baking camembert*' on top. Fold pastry over and trim.

Flip it over so the folds are now on the bottom.

Egg wash, bake, Fan 190, 30 min.

👤 Did someone say calories? This is just the best Christmas food you will ever eat – and it's so easy. Three shop-bought ingredients washed with egg and baked until the cheesy deliciousness oozes out all over your plate. Serve it with a salad dressed with a very sharp vinegary dressing. This is a dinner where afterwards I definitely plan to simply relax on the sofa with the 7yo, hopefully both snuggled up in front of a Christmas movie.

BEETROOT & ONION DHAL

Dice & fry 1 *onion*, 1 clove *garlic*, 10g *ginger* in oil.

Add 2tsp *Madras curry* powder, 150g *red lentils*.

Add 200ml *coconut milk*, 200ml *water*. Simmer 15 min.

Fry 1 sliced *onion* until brown, add 1 tsp *yellow mustard seeds*, ½ tsp *chilli flakes*.

Briefly stir *cooked beetroot* through, top with *natural yoghurt* & onions.

This delicious idea is borrowed from *Nigel Slater*, but I have swapped out his simpler dhal recipe for my own slightly more complex, but favourite dhal. The dhal recipe here is amazing just on its own with rice or flatbreads, but with the additions of beetroot, yoghurt and onion suggested by Nigel, it is just taken over the top to a magical place. It's a wonderful soothing plate of gently spiced comfort food. Make sure you only very briefly stir the beetroot through the dhal at the end, or the whole dish goes pink! The 7yo absolutely adored this – beetroot is his favourite vegetable.

POP's PASTA

🐦 Sweat two thinly sliced *red onions* in *olive oil* until soft.

Add ½tsp *marmite*, ½tsp *flour*, pinch of *salt*.

Add 100mL *water*.

Very gently heat, 30 min, replenish water if needed.

Cook 200g *pasta*, add to sauce.

Finish with a knob of *butter*, *parmesan* & *black pepper*.

👤 Marmite was one of Sam's favourite foods. As he became very ill towards the end, one of the few things he wanted to eat was Marmite on Toast. In fact, the tradition became so established, that we even have an empty jar of Marmite in our memory box. The 7yo likes to take the lid off and sniff it when he is looking through Pop's old things and remembering. This simple supper is therefore a memory box meal, and a big warm umami hug from Pop, in a bowl – that's why in this house, we call it 'Pop's Pasta'.

'Marmite pasta' was popularised by *Nigella Lawson*, but this is actually an adaptation of a recipe from *Anna del Conte* (Italy's version of Delia Smith). The marmite only really adds savour to the dish – if you want it more 'marmitey', just add a bit more.

A QUICK TEA

SPAGHETTI CARBONARA

🐦 Cook 200g *spaghetti*.

Fry chopped *bacon* in *olive oil*. Add diced *shallot* and merest ½ clove *garlic*. Set aside.

Mix 1 *egg*, grated *parmesan*, *black pepper* and 25ml *double cream*.

Drain spaghetti into large bowl, add egg mix & bacon mix. Stir.

Serve with *parmesan* & *black pepper*.

👤 An absolute family favourite, spaghetti carbonara is a mainstay of our kitchen appearing on the menu probably once a month. It's fast, being cooked from start to finish in 15 minutes, and it's tasty. On Twitter, I have had much 'discussion' with Italian friends about my recipe – I *know* it's not authentic – Italians do *not* add cream. But I like a splash, because it makes the sauce silkier, and helps stop the egg scrambling in the hot pasta. I also add a splash of milk to my scrambled eggs and omelettes, so there! If you don't like the addition of cream, just leave it out, and perhaps add an extra egg. Italians also do not use garlic, but again, just the slightest whiff of it really enhances this dish for me. It's a rich dish, so I use plenty of black pepper.

SWEETCORN POPPERS

🐦 Mix 3 cobs of *fresh sweetcorn* kernels, 75g shredded *mozzarella*, 75g *cream cheese*, 2 chopped *spring onions*, ¼ tsp *chilli powder* (opt.).

Add 40g *cornmeal*, 30g *flour*, 1 *egg*.

Shape as balls, coat in mix of 75g *panko breadcrumbs* & 25g grated *parmesan*.

Fry in hot *oil* until golden, 6 min.

👤 Who said vegetarian food can't be a little bit indulgent and even 'dirty'? These poppers are perhaps the best way I have discovered of using up our sweetcorn glut from the allotment and make a simple, and very popular tea for the 7yo. You can deep fry the poppers, or just fry them in a wok with about 1" of sunflower oil. They need to be served with a dressed crunchy salad and some sort of sauce – the one here was a chipotle barbecue relish (out of a jar). This kind of tea is the perfect excuse for buying jars of relish at food festivals. Sam and I always loved going to the food festival in Wetherby with his family, tasting as much as possible and choosing the best produce. Pick your relishes well and they become 'hero ingredients', lifting up your simple tea and making it a little bit special.

LEFTOVER CHICKEN 'ALFREDO'

🐦 Cook 200g *pasta*.

Finely dice ½ *fennel* & *garlic* clove, gently fry.

Add *leftover roast chicken*, heat.

Add 100g grated *cheddar* & 100ml *creme fraiche*.

Use *water* to make sauce desired consistency. Season.

Add cooked pasta, serve.

👤 When you're roasting a chicken for two, there are always leftovers, and they are some of my favourite things to cook with. This is a simple pasta dish perfect for the 7yo to eat in front of cartoons after a hard day at school. On this occasion I used pasta spirals, but I'm not sure they were best suited to the sauce – conchiglie or tagliatelle would probably be better. And a special message to Carmen, my incredible Italian post-doctoral co-worker, I know putting chicken in sauces is not very Italian, and is actually a New York American thing to do! I also know this is a massively shortcut 'Pasta Alfredo' and the use of fennel is a bit weird – that's fine by me, because it tastes great (and surely it's better than the alternative, which is opening a can of Heinz spaghetti hoops)?!

FILLY's BREAD & BUTTER LORRAINE 'EN MUG'

🐦 Melt a knob of *butter* in a mug in microwave.

Tear up 1 slice *white bread* very small. Add 1 **beaten** *egg*, 60mL *milk*, chopped *ham* (or *cooked bacon*), handful grated *cheddar*, *salt & pepper*.

Add to mug, microwave 1.5 min.

Turn out and top with grated *cheddar* while hot.

👤 One of the brilliant things about Twitter is the random connections you make, and the way in which they can enrich your life. Felicity (Filly) is a disability rights activist, who once studied Chemistry at The Open University. She shared this recipe with me, and I thought it was a fantastic thing to feed the 7yo for tea when I was pressed for time. How often do you find a recipe you can cook in a mug in less than 2 minutes, and that a hungry boy will devour and ask if there's another one?

CABBAGE and BACON PASTA

🐦 Fry chopped *smoked streaky bacon*.

Add sliced *cabbage*, *thyme* a knob of *butter*, 1 tbsp *water* & salt.

Heat with lid on until cabbage is soft.

Add cooked *pasta* & cubes of *mozzarella cheese*.

Stir and let cheese start to melt in residual heat.

Drizzle with *olive oil*. Serve.

👤 Pasta dishes are always useful, and this combination of cabbage and bacon is great – flavours we love in this house. It takes 15 minutes from start to finish and is perfect to put down in front of the 7yo for tea. I think I adapted the original idea from *Jamie Oliver*. I suspect it may be even better with *Taleggio* cheese stirred through in terms of flavour, but there is something about the cool milkiness of mozzarella just starting to melt that I adore in the mouth against the crispy bacon bits and the bite of the pasta.

FRENCH DIP

🐦 Oven-cook (or warm through) a *crusty baguette*.

Spread with *horseradish* and load with leftover cold *rare roast beef*.

Serve with *hot gravy*, *Dijon mustard* and *fries*.

👤 OK, so it's 'just' a roast beef sandwich, but with a pot of hot gravy to dip it into, mustard *and* horseradish, and crisp, rustling fries on the side, it's a thing of total beauty. This sandwich was one of Sam's favourite things to eat when we were travelling in the USA. For the baguette, I use one of those part-cooked, bake-in-the-oven ones from the supermarket – in fact these very often fill the role of 'crusty bread' in our house. Purists will tell you the quality of gravy is key, and of course, you could save some of your beautiful handmade roast beef gravy (see page 83) to reheat. But I've made it with Bisto, and it still put a big fat grin on my face.

EGG IN THE HOLE

🐦 Cut hole in a slice of *white bread* with a cookie cutter.

Heat *sunflower oil* in frying pan.

Add *bread* (and 'hole') and start frying.

After almost finishing one side, flip *bread* and add *egg* to hole.

Cook until bottom of *egg* is set & bread golden.

Flip back briefly to seal top of *egg*.

👤 Sam taught me this recipe – I'd honestly never seen it before. It probably takes the highest level of cooking skill of everything in this book! To get the egg, the bread and the 'hole' all perfectly cooked requires exceptional feel, timing and care – you want the egg to be mostly set, but just a tiny bit running in the middle, and the bread to be crisp and golden. You get the idea from the recipe – probably even just from the picture – find your own way of doing it to get it just right. The 7yo thinks it's a fantastic tea (when I get it right). He always says the hole is the best bit!

PAD THAI

To a hot pan, add (in order):

Prawns. Spring onions. Egg.

Then 1tbsp *Fish sauce*, 1-2tbsp *sweet chilli sauce*, very good squeeze *lime juice.*

Add softened ('cooked') *rice noodles*.

Finish with crushed *dry roast peanuts*, *coriander* and lots of *red chilli* (for me).

Prawns are one of the 7yo's favourites, and this Pad Thai is so fast and tasty. It takes longer to get all the ingredients out of the cupboard than it does to cook it. This was always one of Sam's favourite teas as well, and making it is a bit of a ritual. It's become one of those dishes I can just cook without ever really thinking – that kind of cooking is very therapeutic.

PASSION FRUIT MERINGUE

Whip *double cream* until it is just beginning to stiffen.

Place on a *meringue nest* – the very best you can buy.

Top with *passion fruit* pulp.

This is not a recipe, and I know *everyone* does this. It's just a reminder, mostly to myself, that it is possible to get a 'sophisticated' pudding down on the table in less than 5 minutes. Obviously, you can use other fruit on the top - *raspberries* are classic - but somehow, the ability of passion fruit to provide both flavour and a kind of sauce makes it ideally suited to the job. The secret here is to buy the very best meringue nest you can find. It absolutely must *not* be one of those bright white ones that shatters into dust like Plaster of Paris, rather one of the slightly dusky pinkish-brown ones, that yields a fudgy interior. Yes, they cost more, but you are getting pudding in 5 minutes here. If you want to make the meringue nests yourself, just look it up on Google - honestly, this is not really the cookbook for you!

SATURDAY INDULGENCES

P&P PANCAKES, BACON and MAPLE SYRUP

🐦 Dry: 125g *plain flour*, 1tbsp *sugar*, 1tsp *baking powder*, ½tsp *salt*.

Wet: 120g *milk*, 1 *beaten egg*, 25g *melted butter*.

Mix wet into dry, throw in *blueberries* (optional).

Fry in the melted butter pan with *sunflower oil*. Flip when 'holes' appear & bottom golden.

Serve with grilled *streaky bacon* & *maple syrup*.

👤 Every Saturday, we'd always go to The Pig & Pastry for breakfast, before shopping on the local high street – the 'Bishy Road'. We were such regulars that Sam and I even appeared in their cookbook, back in our child-free days when we could relax at the counter with coffee and the papers. The 7yo loves their waffles & bacon. When lockdown came, I wanted to make Saturday mornings at home special. I couldn't master waffles, but I could cook pancakes. Although they have never appeared on the P&P menu, it is what I now cook in homage to them. The bacon must be streaky – the crispness when grilled is perfect. These pancakes are also brilliant served with fruit (*raspberries* or *watermelon*), and *black pudding* makes a great addition to bacon. The quantities will make two frying pans worth of pancakes – 2-3 servings.

FRIED CHICKEN

🐦 Cut *boneless chicken thighs* in half.

Soak all day in *milk* and a squeeze of *lemon* juice (or just *buttermilk* if you have it), with 2tsp *paprika*, 1tsp *dried thyme*, 1 bashed *garlic* clove, *salt*, *pepper*.

Drain, then dredge in flour with similar seasoning blend (no garlic).

Deep fry, 180°C, 8 min.

👤 Fried chicken is deeply comforting and has got me through some very bad times. I swear this stuff is almost as good as what you can get from a well-known takeaway chain. Whenever we visited the USA, Sam, me and the 7yo always went to at least one KFC. I love that in the US, fried chicken is never served with fries, but with mash or mac & cheese – perfect for home cooking. Fried chicken is also great with corn, which we always grow on the allotment.

For *American 'gravy'* just make a white sauce with the *dripping* from the first batch of fried chicken (instead of butter), *flour*, *stock*, *milk*, *salt* & *pepper*.

Another (dirtier) way to enjoy fried chicken is to put it in a good *brioche burger bun* with *sriracha mayo* (literally just 2:1 mayo:sriracha), *jalapenos* and *shredded lettuce*. Even though the 7yo isn't a massive fan of chillies, he goes completely crazy for sriracha mayo!

CHICAGO-STYLE RIBS

🐦 Cook

Dry rub (1tbsp *paprika*, 1tsp *celery salt*, 1tsp *brown sugar*, 1tsp *garlic powder*, ½tsp *dried thyme*, ½tsp *mustard powder*, ¼tsp *white pepper*) on *thick cut pork ribs*, leave 30 min.
Roast, Fan 200, 15 min.
Lower heat to Fan 120, wrap *ribs* in foil, place on a rack above small baking tray of *water*, 1.5-2 h.

🐦 Finish

Brush cooked ribs in BBQ sauce (170g *ketchup*, 25g *black treacle*, 25g *golden syrup*, 60ml *cider vinegar*, 60ml water, ½tsp *salt*, ½tsp *black pepper*). Stand 10 min.
Serve with extra BBQ sauce.

👤 I love ribs. If I was on death row, (and in honesty I've sometimes felt like that since Sam passed away), the dish I would order is a huge slab of ribs, homemade slaw, and a mountain of golden lightly battered onion rings. This ribs recipe is shamelessly adapted from a book I love (*Dirty Food* by *Carol Hilker*). Chicago ribs have both a dry rub and a sauce applied at the end, and it's my favourite way to have them. The recipe may be two tweets – but it's not hard, and it's worth it! It also gives you some leftover barbecue sauce. This kind of home-cooked junk food is my go-to on a Saturday. Slow-cooked perfection to eat in front of an episode of Dr Who with the 7yo.

BEER-BATTERED ONION RINGS

Add 220ml *fizzy cold beer* to 120g *plain flour* & ½tsp *salt*.

Slice *large onion* into rings, coat in flour.

Dip in batter, deep fry in batches in hot oil until crisp & golden.

Drain, season, serve.

I know it may seem strange to include a recipe for a simple side dish – but sometimes, one beautiful thing on a plate can elevate your whole meal to the next level – a 'hero dish'. These onion rings do that. If I have the time and energy, I cook ribs properly from scratch – you can find my favourite recipe on the previous page – but if not, these onion rings will elevate one of those slabs of pre-cooked ribs you can buy from most supermarkets. The alcohol in the beer does cook off, but if you don't want to use beer, just use fizzy ice-cold water.

Gardening was one of Sam's passions, and we have always grown onions on our allotment – they are one of the easiest and most satisfying things to grow. The photograph shows me and the 7yo planting the onion sets. The 7yo always enjoys watching their progress and helping to harvest them. Onion rings are a fantastic way to use larger onions, and (whisper it quietly) I may even prefer them to french fries.

FISH and CHIPS

🐦 Cut large *potatoes* into chips, soak in water.

Drain & dry chips. Dredge *fish* in seasoned *flour*.

Add 200ml *fizzy cold beer* to 125g *plain flour*, 1tsp *baking powder* & ½tsp *salt*.

Deep fry chips 150°C until soft, 6 min, drain.

Dip *cod fillets* in batter, deep fry 180°C, 5-8 min. Keep warm.

Finish chips, 190°C, 2-3 min.

👤 Before lockdown, I'd never made fish and chips – but the chippy was shut, and I craved it. I tried to emulate the amazing meal we ate as a family at Stein's Fish & Chips down in Padstow. The home-made version was so good, I've done it again. I'd recommend Maris Piper potatoes and cod for the fish, but any white fish fillets will work – cooking time depends on thickness. It's really easy, you just slowly crank up the temperature in the deep fat fryer as you go!

When the photo was taken, there were sadly no mushy peas. Sam's family originate from Lancashire, and always make cracking mushy peas. It takes some time and I can never do it as well as them, so for me, opening a can is fine. It's easy to make a quick tartare, simply by putting chopped *capers*, *gherkins* & *parsley* through *mayo* with a squeeze of *lemon juice*.

BUFFALO & BBQ CHICKEN WINGS

Chicken Wings
15 *wings* – discard tips, halve wings at 'elbow' to give mini drumstick & upper wing.
Mix 100g *flour*, ½tsp *paprika*, ½tsp *salt*, ½tsp *black pepper*.
Coat wings in flour, leave 30 min.
Deep fry (180°C, 7 min) & drain.
Melt 50g *butter* in 75ml *Frank's hot sauce*.
Tip wings in sauce, shake, serve.

Sides
Slice *celery* & *carrot* into sticks.
Ranch dressing: 2tbsp *mayo*, 2tbsp *sour cream*, 2 tsp *white wine vinegar*, ¼tsp *salt*, pinch *black pepper*, pinch *garlic powder*, generous fine-chopped *parsley* & *chives*.

Wings are the ultimate Saturday night TV food and bring back so many happy 'bar & baseball' memories of evenings spent with Sam on the road in America (see page 32). It may seem a lot of butter, but you don't eat it all, and anyway, it's delicious and you need it with the vinegary heat of the hot sauce. To make BBQ wings, replace hot sauce with *BBQ sauce* and halve the *butter*. The 7yo is now transitioning from BBQ wings, and steals increasing numbers of the hot wings!

HOMEMADE PIZZA

🐦 Dough
Mix 250g *bread flour*, 250g *plain flour*, 1½tsp *salt*, 1 heaped tsp *dried yeast*.
Add 1tbsp *olive oil*, 325ml warm water, knead (I use a mixer – it's a wet dough).
Place in oiled bowl. Cover 1-2 h until risen.
Knock back. Shape half into 2 pizza bases. Freeze half.

🐦 Topping
Open can *Mutti Pizza Sauce*.
Using a spoon spread a few spoonfuls thinly on the pizza base.
Add your favourite toppings – mine are *salami, black olives, mushrooms & mozzarella*. Scatter a little *parmesan* (or *cheddar*) over.
Cook, Fan 230, 8-10 min.

👤 We love homemade pizza night! I get all sorts of things out of the fridge and cupboards and the 7yo invents his own pizzas – it's anarchic fun. Sam was amazing at throwing parties for the 7yo and his friends after school – the most popular were always his pizza parties (sadly such parties are not in my skillset). I make no apologies for *Mutti pizza sauce*, it's the best shortcut ingredient I know. The dough is *Hugh Fearnley-Whittingstall's* 'magic dough' – it makes everything from breadsticks to loaves, and it freezes.

BEEF & ALE STEW with HORSERADISH DUMPLINGS

Toss 350g *beef shin* in *seasoned flour* – fry in *oil* till brown.

Add 330ml *ale*, 150ml *water*.

Add 1 *onion*, 2 *carrots*, 2 *celery* stalks (all thick sliced), *Worcester sauce, bay leaf, thyme, salt & pepper*.

Fan 140, 3+ h.

Mix 100g *SR flour* 50g *suet*, 1tbsp *horseradish sauce*, 2-3tbsp water, shape.

Fan 180, add dumplings, 15 min. Lid off, 15 min.

When you've been for a wintry outdoor adventure, which is something I often do with the 7yo, there's nothing better than getting back to a house filled with the smell of beef & ale stew. This is a recipe the 7yo can cook some of before going out – giving him something to look forward to as we go exploring a local nature reserve. All you need to do when you get home is pop the dumplings in the top of the casserole and clean off your wellies. Do ask specifically for *shin of beef* ('*stewing steak*' on the butcher's counter in big supermarkets is often shin). It really is the best as it cooks long and slow without ever toughening up. Serve with jacket potatoes or crusty bread.

SWEET and SOUR HAGGIS

🐦 Sweet and Sour
Fry *onion* pieces in *oil*, 2 min.
Add *red pepper*, grated *ginger*, 2 min.
Add small *can pineapple chunks* & juice. Boil.
Add 1 tbsp *light soy sauce*, 1 tbsp *rice vinegar*, 1 tsp *cornflour*.
Shape *haggis* into balls. Dip in *flour*, then batter (2:1 *beer:flour*).
Deep fry 7 min. Add to sauce, serve.

🐦 Egg Fried Rice
Stir fry *egg* (30 sec) in *oil*.
Add *boiled rice*, 1 tbsp *soy sauce* and *peas*.
Fry till rice gets crisp fried bits.

👤 I got more abuse for this recipe on Twitter than any other I have cooked. The bottom line is that in 2020, Burns night and Chinese New Year fell on the same day and I wanted to do a double celebration. It tastes amazing – the spicy haggis goes perfectly with the sweet sauce and is ideally suited to the crisp battered style of take-away sweet & sour. The 7yo adores sweet & sour, and I think this is the best one I've ever made. But if you really can't face it, just replace the haggis with pork. The sauce is adapted from a *Ching-He Huang* recipe, but it is essentially the way it's made in every UK Cantonese takeaway.

LAMB DOPIAZA, SPICED GREEN BEANS

Lamb Dopiaza
Coat 400g *diced lamb* with *black pepper* (lots) & 100g *yoghurt*.
Fry 6 pods of *cardamom seeds*, 1½tsp *coriander seed*, 1½ tsp *cumin seed*. Bash with 1tsp *garam masala*, ½tsp *turmeric*.
Cut 1 *onion* into wedges, fry till brown, remove.
Fry 2 sliced *onions*, 2 cloves *garlic*, 10g *ginger*, 15 min.
Add chopped *red chilli* & spices, 1 min.
Add 1tbsp *tomato puree* & lamb, 4 min.
Add 300ml *water*, simmer, lid on, 1 h.
Reduce sauce until tender, 15 min.
Add onion wedges, ½tsp *garam masala*, serve.

Spiced Beans
Blanch *green beans*.
Fry 1tsp *yellow mustard seed*, 5 *curry leaves*, sliced *green chilli*, 2 min.
Add 50g *desiccated coconut*, 2 min.
Add green beans, ½tsp *garam masala*, salt, 2 min.

Including this dish is a bit of an indulgence, not just a Saturday one, because try as I might, it's un-tweetable! But this *'Hairy Bikers'* recipe is my favourite curry - packed with flavour. Sam and I used to eat curries after putting the 7yo to bed - now the 7yo is increasingly craving them himself (they grow up so fast). Going to the effort with the vegetable side dish really makes it feel 'Saturday' special.

SUNDAY ROASTS

THE HEARTBEAT OF FAMILY LIFE

Roast dinners have been the heartbeat of my family life since I was a child. A roast dinner forces everyone to slow down, it builds a sense of togetherness. So many of my own family memories revolve around Sunday lunch. There was always the anticipation of which meat and sauce we were going to have. My dad sat at the table, carving the meat, while mum bustled round in the kitchen making the gravy. I can even remember running off once the meal was complete to watch Space 1999 on the TV – the start of a life-long sci-fi obsession!

I serve a roast dinner on a big platter. What you see in the photographs is just the first plateful. What you don't see is how the meal goes on, with me and the 7yo stealing our favourite bits off the platter – an extra roast potato (or three), another spoonful of cabbage, a second helping of meat. Proper, greedy, interactive family eating. When Sam was here, part of our Sunday roast tradition was that as he carved, the 7yo would sneak in and Sam would give him the best little bits. I had to pretend I was busy at the cooker and couldn't see – it was their 'secret' little game. In moments like these, families are made.

When cooking a roast, I often choose the vegetables depending on the meat and the season. I think certain vegetables go particularly well with certain roasts. I have tried to capture that through this chapter, which is essentially a series of individual dishes – each condensed into a single tweet. Mix and match them to make your own perfect roast.

As you read, you will see that I always make gravy from roasting pan juices to essentially the same formula – pour off fat, add flour, water/juices/stock/wine, season and add something acidic. Dropping the pH just a little bit always makes a sauce more lip-smacking – you can never quite take the chemist out of the cook!

I must credit Simon and Matthew, the Bishy Road butchers, who consistently supply us with top quality, locally sourced meat. We are only a small family; buying meat from them means we always get the perfect-sized joint for a greedy Sunday roast, with just the right amount of extras for leftovers.

There are two constants on every roast dinner I cook – roast potatoes & Yorkshire puddings. I therefore start with those before considering each different meat in turn.

🐦 Roast Potatoes
Peel & cut *potatoes* into 2-4 pieces, with flat edges & corners (King Edwards are best, Maris Piper good, we grow amazing Blue Danube).
Parboil in salted water until just starting to soften, 8-10 min.
Drain, put back on heat to dry, shake well.
Toss in *sunflower oil*.
Roast, Fan 180, 50-60 min.

👤 Olive oil does not cook hot enough to make great roasties, and while some swear by duck/goose fat (and it does crisp beautifully), I personally find it a bit greasy tasting.

🐦 Yorkshire Puddings (makes 5-6)
Make batter: ½ mug *plain flour*, 1 *egg*, ½ mug *milk:water* (50:50), pinch of *salt* & *white pepper*.
Heat *sunflower oil* in muffin tin (not Yorkshire Pudding tin).
Add batter.
Bake, Fan 180, 30-35 min, turn oven up to Fan 210 for last 10 min (once meat is removed).

👤 I know some say Yorkshire Puddings should only go with roast beef, but they are simply too good not to have more often. Using half milk half water rather than just milk lightens the batter and guarantees you that perfect rise and crisp edges.

ROAST PORK

🐦 Meat

Leg of Pork – Fan 180, 30 min per 500g, then Fan 200, 20 min.

Belly Pork – Put in roasting tin with 200 ml white wine, all wrapped in foil, Fan 140, 2-3 h, then Fan 200, 20-30 min unwrapped.

Crackling – Dry pork skin, season with lots of *salt & pepper* (*fennel seeds* are good too). If it hasn't crackled (often it won't on a small joint), cut off, put back in oven in enamel tin, Fan 210 (with Yorkshire Puddings). If it still won't crackle, put under hot grill, 2 min.

🐦 Vegetables

Roast fennel – cut in wedges, coat in *olive oil & lemon juice*, season. Roast, Fan 180, 25 min.

Braised red cabbage – slice ½ red cabbage, add 1 diced peeled *cooking apple*, 1 tbsp *redcurrant jelly*, 1 tbsp *red wine vinegar*, 20g butter 75ml *water*, simmer 1h.

🐦 Gravy

Pour fat off roasting tin, add 1 tbsp *flour*, stir, add ½ glass *white wine*, reduce, add *water*, stir, *season*, finish with squeeze *lemon juice*.

🐦 Sauce

Apple sauce – 1 *cooking apple*, 2tsp *sugar*, *water*, boil.

👤 This was Sam's favourite roast and is also the 7yo's. Pork *must* have its skin on – without crackling, roast pork is sad.

ROAST BEEF

🐦 Meat
Topside/Silverside – Fan 180, 15/20 min per 500g + 20 min.
Rib – Fan 210, 20 min, then reduce to Fan 160, 15 min per 500g.
Season your *beef* really well with *salt* and plenty of *black pepper*.

🐦 Vegetables
Roast beetroot & balsamic – peel and cut into wedges, place on foil, add *olive oil, balsamic vinegar, thyme, salt & pepper*. Wrap. Roast, Fan 180, 50-60 min, unwrap and finish with a little more *balsamic vinegar*.
Broad beans & bacon – pod, briefly boil, cool, remove outer pale green shells, briefly fry bright green insides in *olive oil* with fried *chopped bacon*.

🐦 Gravy
Pour fat off roasting tin, add 1 tbsp *flour*, stir, add *water*, stir, add juices from carved beef, season with *salt* & generous *black pepper*, finish with a dash of *balsamic vinegar*.

🐦 Sauce
Horseradish sauce – from jar. I tried making it once, but it was awful!
Mustard – Dijon or freshly-made Colman's English.

👤 As a kid growing up, roast beef was definitely my favourite – two reasons: horseradish sauce is just the best, and it was the only time we were allowed Yorkshire Puddings.

ROAST LAMB

🐦 Meat

Leg – Fan 180, 20-25 min per 500g + 20 min.
Shoulder – Fan 150, 40 min per 500g wrapped in foil, then Fan 200, 20 min unwrapped.
Breast – Fan 140, 2-3 h, wrapped in foil, then Fan 180, 30 min unwrapped.

🐦 Vegetables

Roast Parsnip – peel & slice into long wedges, coat in *sunflower oil*, roast with potatoes, Fan 180, 50-60 min. The thin end should be crisp, bitter & almost burnt, the fat end fudgy & sweet.

Asparagus & peas – simply boiled (3 min).

Buttered leeks – slice thinly, gently fry with generous *butter*, *salt* & *pepper* until soft.

🐦 Gravy

Pour fat off roasting tin, add 1tbsp *flour*, stir, add *water*, stir, add juices from carved lamb, *season*, add ½tbsp *redcurrant jelly* and finish with a dash of *balsamic vinegar*.

🐦 Sauce

Mint relish – chopped *mint*, fine chopped *shallot*, 2tsp *caster sugar*, juice of ½ *lemon*, 1tbsp warm *water*. The sauce described here is a thin relish, if you prefer a thicker mint sauce or jelly, buy one.

ROAST CHICKEN

🐦 Meat
Season whole *chicken* well with *salt* and *pepper*, dot skin with *butter*. Stuff with 20g *butter*, wedges of *lemon*, 2 cloves *garlic* and chopped *tarragon*. Roast, Fan 180, 20 min per 500g + 20 min.

🐦 Vegetables
Steamed cabbage – melt large knob of *butter* in pan, add ½ *shredded cabbage*, and 2tbsp *water*, place lid on, steam 5 min until cabbage soft and buttery. Season.

Grandma's Green Beans – just how my Mum cooks them (I always call them 'Grandma's green beans for the 7yo). Make a simple white sauce with *butter, flour, milk, salt & white pepper*, lightly boil *green beans*, drain, pour white sauce over and heat through.

🐦 Gravy
Pour fat off roasting tin, add 1tbsp *flour*, stir, add ½ glass *white wine*, reduce, add *water*, stir, *season*, finish with squeeze of *lemon* juice.

🐦 Sauce
Bread sauce (for special occasions) – heat 10g *butter*, fry 50g *onion*, *thyme*, 2 crushed *cloves*, *bay leaf* & a pinch of *salt*. Add 10g chopped *streaky bacon*. Add 150ml *milk*, simmer. Add 1 slice *white bread* ripped up. Stir & simmer until smooth.

ROAST DUCK

Meat
Prick the *duck* skin all over with a fork, season generously with *salt & pepper*. Roast in tin on rack, Fan 180, 20 min per 500g + 20 min.

Vegetables
Petits Pois a la Francaise – soften sliced *spring onions* in *butter*, add *frozen peas*, 100ml *chicken stock* & shredded *little gem lettuce*. Finish with a knob of *butter, salt & pepper*.

Gravy
Pour fat off roasting tin, add 1tbsp *flour*, stir, add *water*, stir, add juices from carved duck, season with *salt & pepper* and finish with *lemon* juice.

Sauce
Cherry sauce – Soak 75g dried *cherries* in 200ml *red wine*. Add 1tbsp *red wine vinegar*, 25g *sugar*. Simmer 30-60 min and reduce right down to a sticky glossy sauce (add a splash water if you go too far).

My favourite roast – definitely for high days & holidays in this house. I always associate duck with luxury, because this is what we used to have for Christmas Dinner when I was young. The cherry sauce is a *Delia Smith* recipe, and is absolutely incredible – I can't eat roast duck without it!

INDIAN ROAST LAMB

🐦 Meat
Marinade *half leg of lamb* in 200ml *yoghurt*, 6 pods worth of crushed *cardamom seeds*, 2tsp *paprika*, 2tsp *turmeric*, 2 cloves crushed *garlic*, *salt & pepper* for 3+ hours, before cooking as usual (page 84).

🐦 Indian-Spiced Potatoes and Yorkshire puddings
As page 81, but after parboiling, toss in *sunflower oil* with 1tsp *turmeric*, 1tsp *paprika*, 1tsp *cumin*. Roast as usual. Add sliced *onion* for last 15 min. Sensational! I often use them as a side dish. For YPs add *garam masala* (1tsp heaped per 5 YPs) to batter.

🐦 Vegetables
Carrots – boil, drain, add *butter* & toasted crushed *coriander seed*.
Aubergine & Feta – cube, toss in olive oil. Roast, Fan 180, 20 min, add chopped *feta & cherry tomatoes*, roast additional 10 min.

🐦 Gravy
Drain excess fat from spiced pan juices, add 1tbsp *flour*, heat 1 min, add *water*, stir, add dash *balsamic vinegar*, season.

🐦 Sauce
Mint yoghurt - chopped *mint* in *yoghurt*.

👤 I'm not one for messing about with a Sunday Roast, but I honestly think this is great, showcasing how spices can elevate a British classic.

CAKES and PUDDINGS

7yo's BLACKBERRY & APPLE CRUMBLE

Peel, core & chop 2 *cooking apples*.

Add 1-2tbsp *sugar*. Add 2 handfuls *blackberries*.

Rub 120g *flour* and 70g *butter*. Add 60g *sugar* and mix gently.

Put fruit in small tin. Put crumble mix on top.

Bake in oven until golden, Fan 190, 30-40 min.

EAT with *custard*.

Sunday dinner always means a proper home-cooked pudding. Crumble is definitely the king of puddings in our house and appears on the table far more often than any other. It's easy to make and hugely variable according to the seasons – you can pretty much crumble anything once you have mastered the basic recipe. Although rhubarb crumble is my absolute favourite, I've included this one because it was actually made by the 7yo himself, with only a little help. He collected all the produce from the allotment, made the crumble, and then wrote up this recipe himself on the computer as part of his 'home-school' work. If you want to make a larger family crumble, make sure you multiply up the quantities – this will generously serve 2-3.

MUM's BREAD & BUTTER PUDDING

Butter 6 slices *bread*, remove crusts, cut into triangles.

Put in tin, pointy bits upwards, add *sultanas*, a pinch *caster sugar* & *cinnamon* as you go.

Add 1 *egg* & 1 *egg yolk*, 1 tbsp *sugar* to 275ml *milk*. Beat.

Pour over bread, soak.

Sprinkle *caster sugar* & *cinnamon*

Bake, Fan 180, 40 min.

I've tried so many recipes for Bread & Butter Pudding, mostly involving making some sort of fancy custard prior to assembly. Honestly, they are a total faff and often give rubbish results. Ultimately, I went back to making it exactly the same way my Mum would have done! I wasn't disappointed – the souffled bread, with crispy bits pointing upwards, the soft custardy underneath flecked with juicy sultanas. You know it's cooked when its golden and just slightly wobbly – serve it with extra thick double cream. The 7yo ate his portion in record time and went back and stole the rest from the tin.

PEAR TATIN

🐦 Peel 4 *pears*, cut in quarters, remove cores.

In large frying pan, melt 50g *butter*, 50g *sugar*, add 3 *cardamom pods*, 1 *star anise*, ½ *cinnamon stick*. Heat & shake until caramelised.

Add pears, 10 min.

Cool. Arrange pears in circular tin, cut side up, point to centre.

Top with *puff pastry*, tuck in, pierce.

Bake, Fan 180, 30 min.

Turn out.

👤 Honestly, I'm not a great baker, pastry maker or dessert chef and this is one of my go-to puddings. In fact, I cooked it so often, that at one point, Sam asked me not to cook it for a while because he was bored of it! However, it's fabulous, using ripe juicy pears and subtle spices. The only downside is, when you make a small version as I usually do (serves 3-4), the pears are often a little too big for the tin to make a lovely, perfect 'flower' display. I usually cut the tips off, so they fit properly. It doesn't really matter, because the pudding tastes amazing however it looks. 'It all goes down the same way' – as my dad would say. Vanilla ice cream gently melting into the caramel sauce is the perfect easy accompaniment, and in fact, always makes me think of my dad, who loves a good scoop of ice cream on a hot pudding.

MICROWAVE SPONGE PUDDING

🐦 Cream 50g *butter* & 50g *caster sugar*.

Slowly add 1 *egg* & 2tbsp *milk*.

Fold in 50g *SR flour*.

Put 2 large tbsp *curd/jam/syrup* in bottom of well-greased 500 ml microwave-safe bowl.

Add sponge mix on top, cling film over.

Microwave 2 min 45 s. Turn out. Serve with *custard*.

👤 Honestly, the easiest pudding you will ever make – the one in the photograph was made from start to finish by the 7yo, except turning it out at the end. 'Daddy that pudding was awesome – it was insane'. The recipe is infinitely versatile, and you really can put anything in the bottom of the bowl – the one shown is cherry curd, but you can use lemon curd, golden syrup, raspberry jam, honey, apple puree & blackberries. It's a good recipe to showcase a 'hero ingredient' – a spectacularly good curd or jam really makes it special. You can store it in the fridge for a few hours once you have cling filmed it. Of every recipe that I have posted on Twitter, this is the one that most people have told me they have successfully copied.

STICKY TOFFEE PUDDING

Sponge (in mixer):
Mix 50g *butter*, 175g *dark demerara sugar*.
Add 1tbsp *golden syrup*, 2tbsp *treacle*, 2 *eggs*. 1tsp *vanilla extract*.
Add 200g *SR flour*.
Boil 200g *pitted dates* + 300ml water.
Puree, add 1tbsp *baking soda*.
Combine, mix, pour into greased 23cm square tin.
Bake, Fan 180, 45 min.

Sauce and Serve:
Melt together 100g *caster sugar* & 100g *butter*.
Add 200ml *double cream*.
Boil until desired consistency & colour.
Reheat sponge portions in microwave, pour sauce over.
Serve with vanilla ice cream

A member of my research team, Buthaina, came from Saudi Arabia. Every time she went home, she brought back fabulous dates. Most of the time, I used them in sticky toffee pudding. Buthaina understood – she was herself a mum to three kids whilst completing her PhD in my lab! This is a *James Martin* recipe, who adapted it from the inventors of the dish. This recipe serves 6-8 – you can never have too much of a good thing, and the sponge freezes.

CHERRY 'CLAFOUTIS'

🐦 Make Yorkshire Pudding batter – ½ mug *flour*, 1 *egg*, ½ mug *milk:water* (50:50) & a pinch *salt*.

Enrich with 15g melted *butter*, sweeten with 1 tbsp *caster sugar*.

Tip into hot *oiled* dish & drop stoned *cherries* in.

Bake, Fan 200, 30-40 min.

Serve with granulated sugar & vanilla ice cream.

👤 This is probably the most admired recipe I have posted on Twitter – the end result is a thing of beauty, and it is just so simple. It is *not* a proper French cherry clafoutis, which is more involved and requires a sweeter, richer batter. However, having tried to do it the French way, I prefer this – it's certainly easier. When cherries are in season, this is top of my pudding list – I struggle not to eat it all.

GRANDMA's RHUBARB DROP

Make Yorkshire Pudding batter – ½ mug *flour*, 1 *egg*, ½ mug *milk*:water (50:50), and a pinch *salt* (ideally it's just left-over from main course).

Pour into a hot oiled dish and drop in *rhubarb* chopped into 2 cm pieces.

Bake in a hot oven for 30-40 min.

Serve with lots of *granulated sugar*.

I had a really special relationship with my Grandma, and this recipe is the one that takes me straight back to her house. It's a poor man's version of the cherry 'clafoutis' on the previous page (which was already a poor man's version of a real cherry clafoutis). Rhubarb Drop always followed roast beef and Yorkshire Puddings, and the beauty of it is that you don't need to do anything special other than take your standard Yorkshire Pudding batter (make double so there is enough leftover), chop some rhubarb, drop it in and bake. That's it! Serve with *lots* of granulated sugar and I'm happy just with that. You might like some thick double cream too. Eating this, I am once again 7 years old myself, sitting at my Grandma's table, enjoying the best bit of my favourite meal.

HONEY-ROASTED FIGS and HAZELNUT ICE-CREAM

Cut *figs* in half, drizzle with *honey*.

Roast, Fan 180, 20 min.

Toast *hazelnuts* in pan.

Mix and serve with top quality *hazelnut ice cream*.

This is pudding with absolutely no effort, perfect for a summer evening sat in the garden. It relies on two hero ingredients the very best handmade ice cream you can find, and perfectly ripe figs. I love the combination of warm and cold, soft and crunchy, all dripping with sweet sticky honeyed juices. I get my ice cream from Beppe at Trinacria (see page 30), who makes the best ice cream in York. I think a nut flavoured ice cream is perfect for this dish – I used hazelnut, but pistachio would also be good.

SUMMER STRAWBERRY CRUMBLE

🐦 Hull & halve 500g *strawberries*, add 1tbsp *cornflour*. Then add 30g *sugar*, 1tbsp *water*, ½tsp *vanilla extract*.

Mix 60g *flour*, 45g *rolled oats*, 80g *demerara sugar*, ½tsp *baking powder*, ½tsp *cinnamon*, pinch *salt*. Add 45g melted *butter*. Mix.

Put *strawberries* in tin, crumble topping over.

Bake, Fan 180, 30 min.

👤 We grow strawberries on the allotment, and in season there are sometimes more than even the 7yo can greedily eat while we pick them – the photograph shows Sam and the 7yo doing just that. Hunting for ways to use up strawberries, I came across this idea. In honesty, I thought it would be awful, but it was a complete revelation and was added to my list as a different, but delicious, summer pudding. In many ways, I shouldn't have been surprised, we basically love any sort of crumble in this house! This crumble cries out to be topped with good quality vanilla ice cream, rather than custard.

HONEY-ROASTED APRICOTS & CARAMELISED PECANS

Cut *apricots* in half, drizzle with *honey*.

Roast, Fan 190, 15-20 min.

Melt *brown sugar* with a little *water*, add *pecans*, stir until toasted and caramelised.

Mix and serve with the best *vanilla ice cream*.

This is another delicious, simple dessert for a hot summer's day – 20 minutes from beginning to end. You really need the best quality apricots you can possibly find. If your apricots are not so ripe, roast them for longer – they will begin to go soft and yielding. But if your apricots are really good, you don't need to push them so hard, just slightly soften them.

This recipe is super versatile, and you can easily modify the dish to add extra layers of flavour – consider adding *rosemary* or *lavender* to the roasting apricots, or perhaps a *vanilla pod* and some *thyme*, maybe *cardamom* and *saffron*. One word of warning – keep the caramelised pecans away from the 7yo, otherwise they will all be gone before you get to serve up!

BLACKBERRY RIPPLE CHEESECAKE

🐦 Process 350g *digestive biscuits*, add 120g melted *butter*. Press into greased, lined 23 cm flan ring. Fridge, 1h.

Heat 300g *blackberries*, 130g *caster sugar*, Melt sugar, keep fruit as whole as possible.

Whip 350ml *double cream* to soft peaks, fold into 350g *cream cheese*.

Fold in *blackberries* for ripple effect.

Add to base. Fridge, 1h.

Decorate.

👤 The hedgerows on our allotment grow incredible blackberries in huge numbers. In culinary terms this is great, although in gardening terms it creates a constant battle with encroaching thorn bushes. Blackberries this good really deserve to be showcased, and this is an easy, delicious no-bake cheesecake. The only requirements are fresh-picked blackberries and enough space in your fridge! Slice it up using a hot knife – this is a very soft cheesecake. I made this for a big family party, so it serves 6-8 – if you want a smaller one, simply halve quantities, and assemble it in a 16cm flan ring.

BANANA CHOCOLATE CHIP LOAF

In bowl, mash 3 *bananas*, add 75g melted *butter*.

Add 100g *sugar*, 1 beaten *egg*, 1tsp *vanilla extract*, 1tsp *baking soda*, ½tsp *salt*, 185g *plain flour*, stir until smooth.

Add 50g *choc chips*.

Pour in greased loaf tin, top with 30g *choc chips*.

Bake, Fan 160, 50-60 min until skewer comes out clean.

One bowl, one cake tin, one hour, one cake – baking at its simplest. This is a great, straightforward recipe. Believe it or not, the banana loaf in the photograph was made from beginning to end by the 7yo (and mostly eaten by him too). They always say banana loaf should be made with old, ripe bananas, but they never seem to last that long in our house, so I usually have to buy extra, and hide them away to let them over-ripen specially, just so that we can make one of these. It's funny really, because before we adopted the 7yo – our wonderful, special, funny, caring boy – we hardly ate any bananas. Now they are in every shopping basket.

LEMON DRIZZLE LOAF with CANDIED LEMON

Loaf
Beat 170g *butter*, 170g *caster sugar*.
Add 3 *eggs*, mix as you go.
Add 170g *SR flour* & 1 *lemon zest*, mix.
Pour in lined loaf tin.
Bake, Fan 160, 45-50 min, or until skewer comes out clean.
Mix juice of 1 *lemon*, 60g *caster sugar*, prick warm cake all over, drizzle.

Candied lemon
Peel 1 *lemon*, slice into thin strips.
Heat 100g *caster sugar* with 100ml *water*, simmer lemon peel until softened.
Drain, toss in more *sugar* to coat, leave to dry.

Lemon drizzle is my absolute favourite loaf cake – with a cup of tea absolutely nothing could be better. The candied lemon takes it to the next level, but it's a very hard job to stop the 7yo stealing it all off the top.

'YORKSHIRE PUDDING' PUDDING

🐦 Reheat *left-over Yorkshire Pudding* (page 81) in oven, Fan 160, 10 min.

Spoon *golden syrup* over top.

Eat while warm.

👤 This is a totally traditional Northern pudding, eaten after a roast dinner. If you scoff at the idea of leftover Yorkshire puddings, just make sure you bake more than you need in the first place. If you mock the very concept of syrup on a Yorkshire Pudding, then why would you put maple syrup on a pancake? I've sometimes pimped it up for the 7yo with chopped *pineapple*. We often had this at my Grandma's house. Us kids would have golden syrup – it was always a battle to see who could sneak the most from the tin. Grandma preferred homemade raspberry vinegar on hers. Clearly, I'm still just a kid at heart!

CHEF KING'S LOCKDOWN DOUGHNUTS

Mix 100g *SR flour* & 50g *natural yoghurt*. Add 2tbsp *milk* to give very thick batter. Add ½tsp *vanilla extract*.

Deep fry in *oil* until golden.

Mix 25g *granulated sugar* & a shake of *cinnamon* - roll doughnuts.

Microwave *nutella* (30s) to make instant hot chocolate dipping sauce.

Eat warm!

Mr King is the chef at the 7 year old's school. A couple of weeks into the first Coronavirus lockdown, he posted a video of how to make homemade doughnuts from very simple ingredients. The 7yo was able to make them all by himself (obviously with careful supervision using the fryer). I honestly did not believe this recipe would work, because it is so simple – I mean aren't doughnuts supposed to be difficult, needing enriched dough and lots of proving? But, in the words of the 7yo, the doughnuts were 'SENSATIONAL'! I reckon they were better than any doughnuts you can buy from the supermarket. Hats off to Chef King – he's a legend!

A LITTLE LONGER

SPUNTINO's CRISPY PRAWN SLIDERS

🐦 12 Brioche Slider Buns (or 6 Burger Buns)
Rub 250g *bread flour*, 20g *butter*, ¾tsp *salt*. Add 5g *instant yeast*.
Mix ½ beaten *egg*, 1tbsp *milk*, 115ml *warm water*, 1¼tbsp *caster sugar*.
Combine, knead 10 min, leave 1 h.
Shape (70g burgers, 35g sliders) on lined tray, cover, leave 1 h.
Brush with ½ beaten egg/water.
Bake, Fan 180, cup water in extra tray on oven bottom, 15-25 min.

🐦 Prawns
Coat *prawns* in (i) *seasoned flour*, (ii) mix of beaten *egg*, ½tsp *Dijon mustard*, ½tsp *paprika*, (iii) *panko breadcrumbs*.
Fry in hot *oil* until golden brown all over, 2 min. Drain.
Place on sliders with crisp *lettuce*. Dress with best quality *seafood sauce*, perked up with chopped *capers, lemon & Worcester sauce*.

👤 This is adapted from a *Spuntino* recipe – one of our most-loved places. With just over twenty bar stools, around a horseshoe shaped bar on a Soho back street, opposite one of our favourite gay bars – it's the perfect place for high-end American Diner food and great drinks (the best Old Fashioned in London). Spuntino became a standard stop-off for me after science meetings in London, and I later introduced both Sam and the 7yo to its charms. The 7yo loved the little plates of food and the ability to share everything with his two daddies. Sam loved the relaxed friendly vibe, the great cooking and the opportunity to demolish multiple cocktails in a dark corner.

One of my happiest memories is of a weekend away with Sam, with the 7yo safely at his grandparents. We installed ourselves at the counter and ate & drank our way through far too much of the menu before rolling out of the door to go and enjoy the rest of what Soho had to offer. It was just the best of times! I was properly heartbroken when Spuntino closed down this location.

This recipe is exactly the kind of thing I like to cook on a Saturday, when I have a bit more time in the kitchen, and the chance to do some baking. It works in 10 minute bursts – which is ideal for combining with childcare. Basically, it's a lazy version of the 'Prawn Po-Boy' in the Spuntino cookbook. Lazy because I run out of energy when it comes to the dressing (it includes raw egg, which was something Sam was not allowed to eat after his transplant because of his immuno-suppression medication).

I make the buns quite often – they can be filled with all sorts of goodies, and the larger version is an excellent way of making your burgers a bit more special. The length of time you bake the buns for depends on whether you make sliders or burgers. Sliders are perfect kid-sized food – for adults, just eat two or three! I know the recipe for them is a bit more than a single tweet but it's worth it.

P a g e | 106

'ZUNI' CHICKEN on BREAD SALAD

🐦 Chicken: The day before
Season a 1.2-1.5kg *chicken* all over with 2-3 tsp *salt* & *pepper*.
Gently loosen skin on breast & thighs, stuff with *herbs* (*thyme*, *marjoram*, *rosemary* or *sage*).
Twist & tuck wing tips behind shoulders.

🐦 Bread Salad: As oven heats
Cut 250g *farmhouse white bread* (not sourdough) in two, remove crusts.
Brush with *olive oil*, fry to crisp & colour.
Tear into 1-3 inch chunks.
Toss with 3tbsp *olive oil*, 1tbsp *white wine vinegar*, *salt* & *pepper*.
Soak 1 tbsp *currants* in 1tbsp *red wine vinegar* & 1 tbsp warm *water*.

🐦 Cooking (Total: 45-60 min).
Roast chicken, Fan 220, 30 min.
Flip onto breast, 10-20 min.
Flip back for final 5-10 min.
Toast *pine nuts*, add to bread.
Fry 2 cloves *garlic*, 4 sliced *spring onions* in *olive oil*, add to bread.
Drain *currants*, add to bread.
Put bread in baking dish, cover in foil, put in oven last 5-10 min.

🐦 <u>Finishing</u>
Rest chicken.
Pour fat from tin, retain lean drippings. Add 1tbsp *water*.
Slash skin between breast & thigh, drain juice into drippings.
Warm roasting tin – stir, scrape, simmer.
Tip bread on platter, add 1tbsp pan juices, few handfuls of *rocket*.
Cut chicken in pieces, add to platter.

👤 This is my 'Number 1' happiest food memory. Boiling the four-page recipe down into a few simple tweets is total sacrilege – I'm sorry, but I was not going to leave this dish out! I'd been at a chemistry conference in San Francisco, and Sam was with me. One lunchtime, we hopped on the streetcar and headed up towards the Castro – halfway there, we jumped off at the restaurant *Zuni*. We got a walk-in table in the bar area and ordered their famous chicken, which is a two-person sharing dish. It takes an hour to prepare, so we sat and demolished a bottle of wine & some olives – the sun streaming in through the windows and the streetcars rumbling past. We chatted and laughed and just spent the best afternoon ever. And then the chicken came. Just a sublime experience – perfection that will never be matched. Sam cooked this one at home for me when we wanted to recreate the magic – you can see it in the green bowl. I haven't yet been able to face cooking or eating this dish since he died.

HAM in COCA COLA

🐦 Boil *ham* in *Coca Cola* (full sugar) for 1h/kg with 1 *onion* cut in 2.

Remove skin (but not fat).

Make glaze from 1tbsp *black treacle*, 2tbsp *demerara sugar*, 2tsp *powdered mustard*.

Score ham fat, stud with *cloves*, add glaze.

Bake, Fan 200, 15-20 min.

👤 Sam loved Christmas. He loved it so much, that in his final year, he paid for his extended family to get together in a huge house in the Peak District so that we could all spend Christmas together – Christmas dinner for over 20 people. This now-classic *Nigella Lawson* recipe was one of Sam's absolute favourite things to cook (and eat). Every year we would take one to his family's Christmas Eve party. When we all got together in that final year, it was so popular, we had to go out and buy more ham and extra coca cola on Christmas Eve just so that we could make some more for the rest of the holiday.

Every time I cook this now, I think of him. Twitter informs me it's also very good with ginger beer and a ginger marmalade glaze, I've always fancied trying it with Vimto and a cherry glaze. Maybe one day, I'll move on and reinvent the tradition, but for now, making it with Coke somehow tastes like Sam.

LASAGNE

🐦 Meat sauce
Dice & fry 1 *onion*, 1 *carrot*, 2 *celery stalks* in *olive oil*. Remove.
Fry 450g *minced beef* – as it browns, season with *salt, pepper, Italian herbs* & a *bay leaf*.
Add 1 glass *red wine*, reduce. Add cooked veg, can *chopped tomatoes*, ½ can *water*. Simmer 1 h, add water as needed.

🐦 White sauce
Melt 50g *butter*, add 50g *flour*.
Slowly add 750 ml *milk*, stirring to incorporate.
Add *bay leaf*, season with *salt* & *white pepper*. Simmer 10 min.

🐦 Build and bake
3 x (meat sauce, a little white sauce & *parmesan*, layer *pasta sheets*).
Top with white sauce, lots of grated *cheddar* & *parmesan*.
Bake Fan 180, 45 min (until golden).

👤 I don't know what it is with kids and lasagne, but they all seem to absolutely love it. The 7yo is no exception – it's his favourite dinner. It's not really a single twitter recipe – be generous and think of it as three tweets. To be honest, I find making lasagne as much of a pain as trying to explain it concisely. But I really wanted to capture the template of how I do it, because when the 7yo grows up and leaves home, this will probably be the first recipe he turns to when he is feeling sad, or if he wants to impress a girl (or boy).

SITGES PAELLA

🐦🐦 Fry 2 *shallots*, 2 cloves *garlic* in *olive oil*, 5 min.

Add diced small *red & green peppers* (1 of each), 5 min.

Add *squid*, 3 min.

Add 300g *paella rice*, big pinch *saffron*, 750ml *fish stock*, 1tsp *salt*.

Simmer vigorously, 6 min, do not stir, turn pan every 2 min.

Reduce heat, add (e.g.) *raw prawns*, *clams*, *mussels*, push into rice.

Cook 14 min, scatter *peas* over part way through, avoid stirring. All liquid should be adsorbed.

Turn off heat, cover and rest 5 min. Serve with lemon wedges.

👤 Paella was a go-to family dish – this recipe serves 3-4. It always takes me straight back to the seafront in Sitges – one of our favourite holiday destinations. Sitges is a beautiful traditional Spanish town just 30 minutes from Barcelona. It boasts some incredible food and is also an artistic and creative haven for LGBT+ people. We often went there with our gay friends from York – we would travel as a big group and just have the most wonderful time. In later years, we went there with the 7yo – he loved the sunshine, the food, and the beautiful beaches.

Every time we went to Sitges, we always had paella sat out at a seafront restaurant with a view of the water. When we took the 7yo, we ordered a big family paella and all tucked in. At the end of the meal, the waiter came over and said, 'You are not like a normal English family with fish fingers for the children – your son eats proper food with his daddies, it's beautiful'.

But perhaps my most memorable, or at least dangerous, dining experience came two years earlier, in the same restaurant, at almost the same table, with friends. It was 'Fiesta Mayor', and we settled down for paella, knowing that the main parade may come close to the restaurant. Indeed, as the parade came down the street, we could hear the noise and see the lights. As it got closer, we realised that we were going to get front-row seats for the 'fireworks on sticks', spraying out sparks above everybody's heads. The waiters rushed round making sure the tablecloths were not going to get scorched and we sat there, plates full of paella, sparks raining down around us, music pulsing, a true moment of energy and life that fired us up ready for partying into the small hours and beyond.

Sitges really was our place, and after Sam passed away, I went back with a small group of friends for a long weekend. We scattered some of his ashes into the sea from the dramatic cliffs by the side of the church, just as the sun went down.

I haven't cooked paella since. I'm sure I will again, but it's just too resonant for me to really enjoy it yet.

Page | 112

AFTERS

SAM's MOJITO

Pour 40ml *dark rum*, 40ml *light rum*, a dash *angostura bitters*.

Add lightly spanked *mint*, 1 *lime* in wedges, ½tbsp *sugar* & 'muddle'.

Add lots of *crushed ice* and top with a little *soda water* to taste.

"Of all the gin joints, in all the towns, in all the world, he had to walk into mine. Play it once Sam, for old time's sake. Play it Sam. Play *As Time Goes By*."

Casablanca, in Sitges, was Sam's favourite bar in the world. It was a proper old-school bar, where the point of going was not just to drink, but to talk - to meet new people and forge new friendships. The irrepressible gay owners, Brandon & Juan, found unique connections between their customers and mixed the meanest cocktails in town (yes, the measures really are that large - you can always dial it back a little, but Sam would not have approved). To mark Sam's passing they invented this special mojito. We all drank to his memory and shared some of the stories that you can now find in this book, as well as many more that Sam would never want committing to print. Somehow, with his special mojito in hand I could feel him there, and I like to think that part of his spirit now drifts around his favourite haunts in Sitges, drinking, eating and waiting for his friends to go and party with him.

7yo's BLACK CHERRY THICK SHAKE

Blend 3 scoops good *black cherry ice cream* with 300ml *milk*.

Or...

Blend 3 scoops *vanilla ice cream*, 300ml *milk*, 250g stoned *black cherries*.

Serves 2 people topped with *squirty whipped cream* & extra *cherries*.

One of the wonderful things about food is that it helps you build new memories. The first big trip the 7yo and I made after Sam's death took us to Southern California, where I had a scientific conference. We spent several weeks holidaying first, meandering down the Californian coast from Disneyland in Anaheim to San Diego Zoo. At Crystal Cove, we stumbled across a place called *The Shake Shack*, which was just that, a shack, on top of a bluff, overlooking the sea with a fabulous view. After an idyllic morning on the beach, we had the most wonderful lunch. It was a slice of Californian perfection – I just wanted to stop time and do it every day. So now, we can make black cherry shakes at home and transport ourselves back there. The memory is ours, it's special, and it helps us look to the future, while holding on to the past.

INDEX

A

Apples
    7yo's blackberry & apple crumble, 89
    Apple sauce (side dish), 82
Apricots
    Duck and apricot wraps, 20
    Honey-roasted apricots and caramelised pecans, 98
Artichokes
    Seabass traybake (variation), 39
Asparagus
    Gnocchi with steak and asparagus, 31
Aubergine
    Aubergine & feta (side dish), 87
    Halloumi fingers and aubergine mash, 53

B

Bacon
    Cabbage and bacon pasta, 63
    Filly's bread & butter Lorraine 'en mug', 62
    P&P pancakes, bacon and maple syrup, 69
    Spaghetti carbonara, 59
Bananas
    Banana chocolate chip loaf, 100
Beans
    Duck and cannellini beans, 25
    Kale & cannellini bean stew, 51
Beef
    Beef & ale stew with horseradish dumplings, 76
    French dip, 64
    Lasagne, 110
    Roast beef, 83
Beer
    Beef & ale stew with horseradish dumplings, 76
    Beer-battered onion rings, 72
    Fish and chips, 73
    Sweet & sour haggis, 77

Beetroot
    Beetroot & onion dhal, 56
    Pigeon, beetroot and hazelnut salad, 21
    Quail egg, beetroot and black pudding salad, 16
    Roast beetroot & balsamic (side dish), 83
Black pudding
    Pancakes (variation), 69
    Quail egg, beetroot and black pudding salad, 16
Blackberries
    7yo's blackberry & apple crumble, 89
    Blackberry ripple cheesecake, 99
    Partridge with blackberries and juniper, 17
Blueberries
    P&P pancakes, bacon and maple syrup, 69
Bread
    Bread sauce (side dish), 85
    Deep-fried tortilla (side dish), 42
    Egg in the hole, 65
    Filly's bread & butter Lorraine 'en mug', 62
    French dip, 64
    Grilled sumac lamb and pitta chips, 18
    Mum's bread & butter pudding, 90
    'Zuni' chicken on bread salad, 107
Broad beans
    Broad beans & bacon (side dish), 83

C

Cabbage
    Cabbage and bacon pasta, 63
    Pork tonkatsu, 11
    Steamed cabbage (side dish), 85
Camembert
    Baked camembert and cranberry, 55
Capers
    Quick tartare (side dish), 73
    Sauce vierge (side dish), 39
    Sole meuniere with fries, 37

Carrot
- Beef & ale stew with horseradish dumplings, 76
- Celery, carrot and ranch dip (side dish), 74
- Coriander carrots (side dish), 87

Cauliflower
- Cauliflower cheese pasta, 52
- Chicken and cauliflower cheese, 19

Celery
- Beef & ale stew with horseradish dumplings, 76
- Celery, carrots and ranch dip (side dish), 74

Cheddar
- Cauliflower cheese pasta, 52
- Filly's bread & butter Lorraine 'en mug', 62
- Lasagne, 110
- Leftover chicken 'alfredo', 61

Cheese
- Baked camembert and cranberry, 55
- Cauliflower cheese pasta, 52
- Cheese & onion tart, 50
- Filly's bread & butter Lorraine 'en mug', 62
- Halloumi fingers and aubergine mash, 53
- Lasagne, 110
- Leftover chicken 'alfredo', 61
- 'Smoky' autumn pasta, 47
- Sweetcorn poppers, 60

Cherries
- 7yo's black cherry thick shakes, 115
- Cherry 'clafoutis', 94
- Cherry sauce (side dish), 86

Cherry tomatoes
- Aubergine & feta (side dish), 87
- Cod tricolore, 35
- Italian sea bream, 44

Chicken
- 'Zuni' chicken on bread salad, 107
- BBQ chip chos 1331, 22
- Buffalo & bbq chicken wings, 74
- Chicken and cauliflower cheese, 19
- Chicken and chickpea madras pie, 28
- Chicken and mushroom pie, 27
- Fried chicken, 70
- 'Jerusalem' chicken, 24
- Leftover chicken 'alfredo', 61
- Roast chicken, 85
- Roast chicken and mayo, 15
- Saffron & chilli grilled chicken, 10
- Stu's healing Italian chicken meatball pasta, 26

Chickpeas
- Chicken and chickpea madras pie, 28
- Chorizo and chickpea Stew, 8

Chocolate
- Banana chocolate chip loaf, 100
- Chef King's lockdown doughnuts, 103

Chorizo
- Chorizo and chickpea stew, 8

Clams
- Sam's Mexican fish stew, 42
- Sitges paella, 111

Coca cola
- Ham in coca cola, 109

Coconut
- Lamb dopiaza and spiced green beans, 78

Cod
- Cod tricolore, 35
- Fish and chips, 73

Courgette
- Herb-rolled salmon, 41

Couscous
- Saffron and chilli grilled chicken, 10

Crab
- Whitby crab cakes, 43

Crackling
- Roast pork, 82

Cranberries
- Baked camembert and cranberry, 55
- Duck leg with sweet & sour cranberries, 29

Cream cheese
- Blackberry ripple cheesecake, 99
- Sweetcorn poppers, 60

Cucumber
- Mackerel, rhubarb and cucumber, 36
- Quick pickled cucumber (side dish), 18

Curd
- Microwave sponge pudding, 92

D

Dates
    Sticky toffee pudding, 93
Dhal
    Beetroot & onion dhal, 56
Duck
    Duck and apricot wraps, 20
    Duck and cannellini beans, 25
    Duck leg with sweet & sour cranberries, 29
    Roast duck, 86

E

Egg
    Cherry 'clafoutis', 94
    Egg fried rice (side dish), 77
    Egg in the hole, 65
    Filly's bread & butter Lorraine 'en mug', 62
    Grandma's rhubarb drop, 95
    Mum's bread & butter pudding, 90
    P&P pancakes, bacon and maple syrup, 69
    Pad thai, 66
    Pork ramen, 13
    Quail egg, beetroot and black pudding salad, 16
    Spaghetti carbonara, 59
    Yorkshire puddings (side dish), 81

F

Fennel
    Italian meatball & fennel spaghetti, 30
    Italian sea bream, 44
    Leftover chicken 'alfredo', 61
    Roast fennel (side dish), 82
    Salmon, fennel and dill 'en papillote', 38
    Sea bass, olives and fennel, 45
Feta
    Aubergine & feta (side dish), 87
    Red pepper & feta (side dish), 23
Figs
    Honey-roasted figs and hazelnut ice cream, 96

Flour
    Beef & ale stew with horseradish dumplings, 76
    Beer-battered onion rings, 72
    Brioche slider buns (or burger buns), 105
    Chef King's lockdown doughnuts, 103
    Cherry 'clafoutis', 94
    Fish and chips, 73
    Grandma's rhubarb drop, 95
    Homemade pizza, 75
    'Magic dough', 75
    P&P pancakes, bacon and maple syrup, 69
    Sweet & sour haggis, 77
    Yorkshire puddings (side dish), 81
Fries
    BBQ chip chos 1331, 22
    French dip, 64
    Sole meuniere with fries, 37

G

Gnocchi
    Gnocchi with steak and asparagus, 31
    Mushroom & sage gnocchi, 54
    Summer gnocchi salad, 48
Green beans
    Grandma's green beans (side dish), 85
    Lamb dopiaza and spiced green beans, 78
    Seared tuna 'Nicoise', 40
Gruyere
    Cheese & onion tart, 50

H

Haggis
    Sweet & sour haggis, 77
Halloumi
    Halloumi fingers and aubergine mash, 53
    Halloumi roast vegetables, 49
Ham
    Filly's bread & butter Lorraine 'en mug', 62
    Ham in coca cola, 109

Hazelnuts
- Mackerel, rhubarb and cucumber, 36
- Pigeon, beetroot and hazelnut salad, 21
- Quail egg, black pudding and beetroot salad, 16

Honey
- Honey-roasted apricots and caramelised pecans, 98
- Honey-roasted figs and hazelnut ice cream, 96

Horseradish
- Beef & ale stew with horseradish dumplings, 76

Hot sauce
- Buffalo & bbq chicken wings, 74

I

Ice cream
- 7yo's black cherry thick shake, 115

J

Jam
- Microwave sponge pudding, 92

Jerusalem artichokes
- 'Jerusalem' chicken, 24

K

Kale
- Kale & cannellini bean stew, 51

L

Lamb
- Grilled sumac lamb and pitta chips, 18
- Icelandic lamb chops, 23
- Indian roast lamb, 87
- Lamb dopiaza, 78
- Roast lamb, 84
- Youtuber's lamb and mint curry, 14

Leek
- Buttered leeks (side dish), 84

Lemon
- Lemon drizzle loaf with candied lemon, 101

Lentils
- Beetroot & onion dhal, 56

Lettuce
- Petits pois a la Francaise (side dish), 86

Lime
- Sam's mojito, 114

M

Mackerel
- Mackerel, rhubarb and cucumber, 36

Marmite
- Pop's pasta, 57

Mayonnaise
- Celery, carrot and ranch dressing, 74
- Quick tartare (side dish), 73
- Roast chicken and mayo, 15
- Sriracha mayo (dise dish), 70

Meringue
- Passion fruit meringue, 67

Mint
- Mint relish (side dish), 84
- Sam's mojito, 114
- Youtuber's lamb and mint curry, 14

Mozzarella
- Cabbage and bacon pasta, 63
- Cod tricolore, 35
- Homemade pizza, 75
- *Open tart (variation)*, 50
- Sweetcorn poppers, 60

Mushrooms
- Chicken and mushroom pie, 27
- Mushroom & sage gnocchi, 54
- Professor Dave's steak frites, 9
- Sea bass traybake, 39

Mussels
- Moules mariniere, 34
- Sitges paella, 111

N

Noodles
- Pad thai, 66
- Pork ramen, 13

O

Olives
- Italian sea bream, 44
- Sea bass, olives and fennel, 45
- Seabass traybake (variation), 39

Onions
- Beer-battered onion rings, 72
- Beetroot & onion dhal, 56
- Cheese & onion tart, 50
- Lamb dopiaza, 78

Onions (red)
- Pop's Pasta, 56, 57

P

Parmesan
- Cauliflower cheese pasta, 52
- Cheese & onion tart, 50
- Chicken and cauliflower cheese, 19
- Homemade pizza, 75
- Kale & cannellini bean stew, 51
- Lasagne, 110
- Spaghetti carbonara, 59
- Sweetcorn poppers, 60

Parsnip
- Roast parsnip (side dish), 84

Partridge
- Partridge with blackberries and juniper, 17

Passion fruit
- Passion fruit meringue, 67

Pasta
- Cabbage and bacon pasta, 63
- Cauliflower cheese pasta, 52
- Italian meatball & fennel spaghetti, 30
- Lasagne, 110
- Leftover chicken 'alfredo', 61
- Pop's pasta, 57
- 'Smoky' autumn pasta, 47
- Spaghetti carbonara, 59
- Stu's healing Italian chicken meatball pasta, 26

Pastry
- Baked camembert and cranberry, 55
- Cheese & onion tart, 50
- Pear tatin, 91

Pears
- Pear tatin, 91

Peas
- Petits pois a la Francaise (side dish), 86

Pecans
- Honey-roasted figs and caramelised pecans, 98

Peppers
- Halloumi roast vegetables, 49
- Red pepper & feta (side dish), 23
- Seabass traybake (variation), 39
- Sitges paella, 111
- Sweet & sour haggis, 77

Pigeon
- Pigeon, Beetroot and Hazelnut Salad, 21

Pineapple
- Sweet & sour haggis, 77
- 'Yorkshire pudding' pudding (variation), 102

Pork
- Coffee-brined pork chop, 12
- Pork ramen, 13
- Pork tonkatsu, 11
- Roast pork, 82

Potatoes
- Champ mash (side dish), 17
- Halloumi roast vegetables, 49
- Indian-spiced potatoes (side dish), 87
- Mashed potatoes (side dish), 41
- Parmentier potatoes (side dish), 23, 29
- Roast potatoes (side dish), 81
- Sam's Mexican fish stew, 42
- Sea bass traybake, 39

Prawns
- Pad thai, 66
- Sam's Mexican fish stew, 42
- Sitges paella, 111
- Spuntino's crispy prawn sliders, 105

R

Radishes
- Sam's Mexican fish stew, 42
- Summer gnocchi salad, 48

Raspberries
- Meringue (variation), 67
- Pancakes (variation), 69

Red cabbage
- Braised red cabbage (side dish), 82

Rhubarb
   Grandma's rhubarb drop, 95
   Mackerel, rhubarb and cucumber, 36
Ribs
   Chicago-style ribs, 71
Rice
   Egg fried rice (side dish), 77
   Pork tonkatsu, 11
   Sitges paella, 111
Rum
   Sam's mojito, 114

S

Saffron
   Saffron & chilli grilled chicken, 10
   Sitges paella, 111
Sage
   Mushroom & sage gnocchi, 54
Salmon
   Herb-rolled salmon, 41
   Salmon, fennel and dill 'en papillote', 38
Sausage
   Barbecued hot dog, 32
   Italian meatball & fennel spaghetti, 30
   Stu's healing Italian chicken meatball pasta, 26
Sea bass
   Sam's Mexican fish stew, 42
   Sea bass traybake, 39
   Sea bass, olives and fennel, 45
Sea bream
   Italian sea bream, 44
Sole
   Sole meuniere with fries, 37
Spaghetti
   Spaghetti carbonara, 59
Spinach
   Pork ramen, 13
Squid
   Sitges paella, 111
Steak
   Gnocchi with steak and asparagus, 31
   Professor Dave's steak frites, 9

Strawberries
   Summer strawberry crumble, 97
Sultanas
   Mum's bread & butter pudding, 90
Sweet potato
   Halloumi roast vegetables, 49
Sweetcorn
   Chicken and sweetcorn pie (variation), 27
   Sam's Mexican fish stew, 42
   Sweetcorn poppers, 60
   Sweetcorn relish, 43
Syrup (golden)
   Chicago-style ribs, 71
   Microwave sponge pudding, 92
   Sticky toffee pudding, 93
   'Yorkshire pudding' pudding, 102
Syrup (maple)
   P&P pancakes, bacon and maple syrup, 69

T

Tomatoes
   Chorizo and chickpea stew, 8
   Italian meatball & fennel spaghetti, 30
   Lasagne, 110
   Open tart (variation), 50
   Sam's Mexican fish stew, 42
   Sea bass, olives and fennel, 45
   Seared tuna 'Nicoise', 40
   Stu's healing Italian chicken meatball pasta, 26
   Summer gnocchi salad, 48
   Youtuber's lamb and mint curry, 14
Treacle
   Chicago-style ribs, 71
   Ham in coca cola, 109
   Sticky toffee pudding, 93
Tuna
   Seared tuna 'Nicoise', 40

W

Watermelon
   Pancakes (variation), 69

Printed in Great Britain
by Amazon